Charlemagne

A Captivating Guide to the Greatest Monarch of the Carolingian Empire and How He Ruled over the Franks, Lombards, and Romans

Free Bonus from Captivating History
(Available for a Limited time)

Hi History Lovers!

Now you have a chance to join our exclusive history list so you can get your first history ebook for free as well as discounts and a potential to get more history books for free! Simply visit the link below to join.

Captivatinghistory.com/ebook

Also, make sure to follow us on Facebook, Twitter and Youtube by searching for Captivating History.

Right action is better than knowledge; but in order to do what is right, we must know what is right.

- Charlemagne

Contents

Introduction

Warrior. Ruler. Patron of the arts and language. Terrorist. Brutal oppressor. Protector of the good. Guardian of Christendom. Father of Europe. There are so many different ways in which Charlemagne can be described, and yet the man himself is often seen as an enigma. Depending on the viewpoint of history, he could have been either a monster or a guardian angel. Yet, as with most men, the truth lies somewhere in between. The truth is that he was human.

Charlemagne, crowned emperor of Rome and king of the Franks and Lombards, was the third ruler of the Carolingian Dynasty. He is also known as Charles the Great, and greatness certainly is a fitting word to describe his illustrious rule of 47 years. He added huge tracts of land to the Frankish kingdom, reformed everything from administration to currency to language, and changed the dynamics between the church and state forever—a defining influence on the entirety of Europe during the Middle Ages.

But Charlemagne also lived as a human being, a man who loved, lost, made mistakes, and endured the full spectrum of emotions. A man who was never truly satisfied with his achievements, whose constant thirst for more was never satiated. Although he longed for more, it is safe to say that he will forever remain as one of the most influential figures throughout all of history. And this is his story.

Chapter 1 – Before the Great King

The name of Charlemagne is one that will ring familiar to many, a name that has been invoked by many powers in the centuries since he reigned, from the Holy Roman Empire to Nazi Germany. We all know that Charlemagne was some great king of France. What many don't realize is that Charlemagne was the king of France before the name of France even existed.

In truth, Charlemagne was the king of a far greater territory than modern-day France, one which encompassed six modern countries of Western Europe. This territory was known as Gaul. And the people that Charlemagne ruled would eventually give their names to the land we know as France today. They were called the Franks, and their history stretches back centuries before their first great king was born.

An Early History of the Franks

No one really knows how long ago the Frankish tribe began. Our first records of them come from the time of the ancient Romans, who sought to conquer these people; by that time, the Franks were already a large, efficient, and warlike tribe. They probably originated somewhere in northwest Germany along the banks of the Rhine when a group of smaller tribes came together—perhaps uniting against a common enemy—and formed a confederation. Thus, ruled by two powerful families named the Ripuarians and the Salians, the Franks were born.

They didn't call themselves the Franks, though. This name was given to them by the Romans, and it meant "ferocious," a title that they earned in blood. When Rome expanded into Gaul throughout the first few centuries CE, they became the first people to make lasting records of the Franks, and they clashed with a tribe of "barbarians" that proved to be far more organized than the Romans had expected. Even at the height of its imperial power, Rome may have striven hard against the Franks and even conquered Gaul, but they couldn't seem to stamp out the Franks' fighting spirit. In 287 CE, the Romans had no choice but to sign a treaty with the Franks, which ended in the recruitment of many Frankish soldiers into the Roman army.

The Romans soon discovered that the Franks made far better friends than enemies. In fact, the Franks, fighting on the side of Rome, proved to be such strong soldiers that their Roman colleagues began to make up legends about them. The most enduring of these legends is that the Franks were descended from Trojan warriors. Troy, in its time, had been legendary for its prowess. Romantic as this idea may be, sadly, it's highly unlikely to be true.

Nonetheless, the Franks became an integral part of ancient Rome's mighty army. Within the next 200 years, the number of Franks in the Roman army grew so much that they outnumbered all other soldiers who were not Roman citizens. This turned out to be a good thing. The Franks would become an invaluable asset in Rome's fight against one of history's most intimidating characters: Attila the Hun.

The Huns were a nomadic tribe from Asia and Eastern Europe that had been growing quietly in the shadows for decades by the time that Attila became their king in 445 CE. Attila loved hunting, drinking, and women. He also loved conquest, and unlike the Hunnic kings that had gone before him, Attila had a greater ambition than simply ruling a handful of tribes. In the next six years, he managed to unite the wild and warlike Huns into a single unstoppable force that would bring devastation to the very doorstep of the Roman Empire.

It all started with a beautiful girl named Honoria. As the sister of Roman Emperor Valentinian III, Honoria was a princess of Rome. She was one of the most important women in the world, but her opinion was of no importance whatsoever, especially when it came to whom she would marry. Valentinian wanted to marry her off to a boring old Roman officer for the sake of strengthening family ties. Hating the idea, Honoria decided that she would find herself another husband, one that could make even Valentinian quake in his boots. She wrote a letter to Attila the Hun, enclosing a ring and proposing marriage.

Honoria's bid to control her own fate was short-lived. As soon as Valentinian found out, he promptly married her off to the Roman officer anyway, but it was too late to stop Attila. He'd been promised a Roman princess for his bride, and he would have her, no matter what. Invading Gaul, he began to sack city after city, burning them down in a bid for Honoria.

Much of Gaul itself was a part of Roman territory at the time, but the Franks and their neighbors, the Goths and the Visigoths, were free people, and the Romans faced harsh defeats against Attila before they realized that their only hope of beating him was to fight fire with fire (or barbarians with barbarians, in this case). Roman General Flavius Aetius, a gifted, if prejudiced strategist, formed an alliance with numerous Gallic tribes. The Franks were among them. They came to the aid of the besieged city of Orléans, forcing Attila to abandon the siege and begin a slow flight back toward his homeland. It was a flight he could not sustain. His army ran out of food and water, and having no choice, Attila turned to face the oncoming Romans and their barbarian allies.

Bolstered by their Frankish allies, the Romans came face to face with their Hunnic adversary on the Catalaunian Plains in 451 CE. The battle that resulted was an utterly brutal one for the Franks. Aetius favored his Roman soldiers and viewed barbarians as expendable, so he sent the Franks into horrific danger, resulting in high Frankish casualties while the Romans stayed in comparative safety. Nonetheless, the Franks were fearless, earning their name of "ferocious" as they fell upon the flanks of the Huns. Attila was put to flight again that day, and it was the only time he would ever be defeated.

Attila did not return to Gaul. He was likely planning to do so, but in 453 CE, the Hunnic king met with an unlikely end for such a warlike man. Being polygamous, Attila decided that if he couldn't have Honoria at the moment, he'd simply take a consolation prize to tide him over before he could claim his Roman princess. This proved to be a girl named Ildico, and she would be the death of him—literally. On their wedding night, Attila drank himself into a coma. As he lay in his drunken stupor, his nose began to bleed. The bleeding was not catastrophic, but his drunken state was, for he'd slipped so deeply into an alcoholic coma that he couldn't even sense the fact that his own blood was steadily trickling into his windpipe. Attila drowned in his own blood that night.

The Rise of Clovis

At the time of the Battle of the Catalaunian Plains, the Franks were led by their king, Merovech. His name would become legendary not because of his role in the defeat of Attila the Hun, but because of the grandson he'd leave behind after his death: Clovis.

Merovech's son, Childeric I, died thirty years after the defeat of Attila, leaving the Frankish people in the hands of his son, Clovis, who was only fifteen years old at the time. It was an era in which child rulers often caused terrible grief and trouble for their subjects. A fifteen-year-old, in the modern day, would hardly be considered a suitable ruler for an entire tribe of people. The Franks had much to fear, such as their king growing up into a tyrant or, perhaps worse, a squabbling regency that could erupt into a civil war. But, unlike many others in history, this teenage king would grow into a mighty ruler.

Clovis proved to be a fearless warrior and an adept strategist. He came to power with an ambitious vision: to see all of Gaul united underneath his rule. The only trouble was that Gaul wasn't even under Frankish rule at the time. Instead, it belonged to the Romans.

As evidenced by Flavius Aetius's treatment of the Franks during the Battle of the Catalaunian Plains, Romans may have lived alongside the Franks, but they still believed that they were deeply inferior to the Romans. This prejudice was evident all over the Roman Empire, and Clovis had had enough of it. He must have heard his father's stories of how his men had been butchered like pigs on the plains while the Roman soldiers watched. Clovis was done with Roman rule.

In 486, when he was just twenty years old, Clovis turned on his erstwhile ally, Syagrius, the Roman governor of Gaul. Syagrius met Clovis in an open battle and was soundly defeated by the young Frankish king. The governor fled to another "barbarian" ally, Alaric II, the king of the Visigoths (not to be confused with his great-grandfather, Alaric I, the man who sacked Rome). It proved to be an unwise move. The Visigoths had been killed on the Catalaunian Plains just as the Franks had; besides, Alaric had no intentions of angering Clovis. When Clovis sent messengers to him demanding that he hand over the Roman governor, Alaric was quick to comply. Syagrius was sent to Clovis, who promptly beheaded him. And so, the Roman control of Gaul came to a resounding end. In fact, the entire Roman Empire was in its death throes by this point, and Clovis's killing of Syagrius was one of the final blows that would be struck to the dying empire.

Now that the Romans were out of the way, Clovis set about uniting the whole of Gaul under his rule, conquering those Frankish leaders who dared to stand against him. He killed many of them, forcing their tribes to join him and forming Gaul into a single powerful territory under one Frankish king. By the beginning of the 6th century, Clovis controlled everything from the British Channel to the Alps. His territory included modern-day France, Luxembourg, Germany, and the Netherlands, as well as parts of Switzerland and northern Italy.

Clovis, like generations of Franks before him, was a pagan; he served numerous traditional gods, just as his ancestors had. But for the past 500 years, a new name had been spreading throughout the world from its birthplace in the Middle East. Even Rome had abandoned its gods and astronomers to follow this religion. It was Christianity, and it was spreading slowly over the known world.

Clovis had come into contact with some forms of Christianity during his rule. Not only had he known Romans, who were Catholic, but he'd also met with the Goths, who followed Arian Christianity. Clovis had no quarrel with the Christians, but he had no intention to convert either. But according to his biographer, all that changed during a battle with the Alemanni tribe around 503 CE.

Clovis Converts

The Alemanni were winning.

Clovis's troops were engaged in full battle with the Germanic tribe, which Clovis was trying to beat into submission, a tribe whose lands he'd hoped to add to his growing territory. Now, though, it seemed as if the Alemanni were not simply going to resist him: they were going to destroy him. Wherever Clovis looked, he could see his men were dying.

Clovis was by no means inexperienced in battle. He'd been king for more than twenty years, and he'd spent every one of those years fighting against some enemy, usually an enemy of his own making. But he'd never seen things this dire before. He knew that he was about to be routed, perhaps even killed, and the earth had been stained blood red as his men died right and left. His own blade ran scarlet with blood, and yet more and more enemies came wherever he looked.

He knew that he might not make it home this time, not from this campaign, and his heart fled back to the woman he loved: the

Burgundian princess he'd married. Clotilde, like most of her people, was a Catholic. They were happily married, but there was one thing they'd never agreed on: religion. For years, she'd been imploring him to turn from his traditional faith and serve her God. Clovis had always refused. But now, it seemed that his gods had abandoned him. They seemed powerless in the face of the raging Alemanni.

Clovis was desperate. He wanted to get home, by any means necessary, and he prayed aloud to the God his wife served. Incredibly, before his very eyes, a miracle happened. The tide of the battle began to turn. The Alemanni threw down their weapons, turned their backs, and fled as though the Franks had fallen upon them with chariots of fire.

Or so goes the story of Clovis's conversion as told by Gregory of Tours, a historian from the late 6th century. According to Gregory, Clovis returned to Clotilde, utterly humbled. Once he'd told her everything that had taken place during the battle, Clotilde convinced the Catholic bishop of Reims to preach to Clovis. Many conversations took place between the two men, and in the end, Clovis converted. He was baptized inside a small abbey in Reims, and so the Franks became a Catholic people, or at least their king did.

Regardless of how accurate Gregory's account is, Clovis most certainly did convert to Christianity, namely to Roman Catholicism. He had defeated the Romans nearly twenty years before, but now he adopted the religion of his enemies. And so began the long and complicated history of the Roman papacy and the Frankish kings.

The Merovingian Dynasty

Clovis was more than just a king and a conqueror. He was the founder of a dynasty known as the Merovingian dynasty, named after Clovis's grandfather.

By the end of Clovis's reign, Gaul—and the Frankish people—had become one of the most important powers of Western Europe. The Western Roman Empire had fallen, with its last emperor deposed in

476; by the end of the 5th century, even the last twitches of its corpse had faded. The resulting vacuum was quickly filled by the Eastern Roman Empire and, increasingly, by the rising might of Gaul. This power would be a long-lived one.

Clovis, however, would not share the same happy fate. He died in 511 at his capital, Paris, apparently of natural causes. The empire he'd forged would stand for centuries, and the dynasty he'd founded would rule Gaul for over 200 years.

The Merovingian dynasty governed Gaul from the time of Clovis in the late 5th century to the rise of the Carolingian dynasty—whose most famous king we'll be studying in this book—in the 8th century. Known as the "long-haired kings" for their unique appearance, the Merovingians soon made a name for themselves as being adept and powerful rulers who unfortunately often resorted to simple tyranny.

The spread of Christianity over Western Europe did not come as easily as the snap conversion of Clovis I. Once the Merovingians had closely allied themselves to the Roman papacy, they realized that the papacy was emerging as a greater power than the empire in which it had been born. The title of Western Roman Emperor had faded into oblivion, but the title of Roman Catholic Pope was one that began to command respect throughout Europe. The Merovingians saw him as a useful ally, and they were determined to bring their realm under Catholic control, often for purely political reasons.

Thus, the Merovingians forced evangelism with the edge of the sword, persecuting the pagans that still observed ancient Frankish traditions. As their control over the realm grew, and as other nations began to show the mighty Franks more and more respect over the next 200 years, the Merovingians' appetite for power became insatiable. Their actions were motivated solely by politics, and this would eventually prove to be their downfall.

After years of closely allying with the papacy, the Merovingian kings began to appoint secular leaders in church positions. Laymen performed religious duties, something that the Roman Catholic

Church did not tolerate. Clashes with the papacy ensued, and by the beginning of the 8th century, the Merovingians' long-standing alliance with the pope had all but ended.

A number of other factors contributed to the decline of Merovingian power, and the once-great long-haired kings had become so lackadaisical and feeble that they were now known as the "do-nothing kings." Rome's power was gone, and the papacy itself was threatened. The time was ripe for a new ruler to rise in Western Europe and bring unity back to the scattered people. And that ruler would be a Frankish king.

Chapter 2 – Rise to Power

Illustration I: An equestrian statue of Charlemagne in Paris near Notre-Dame Cathedral.

With the Merovingians' hands tied, Francia—the country that had risen as the home of the Franks when Clovis's Gaul gradually shattered into numerous small kingdoms—nonetheless needed to be governed. Power did not simply disappear when the Merovingian rulers gave it up. Instead, it dissipated into the hands of others, namely, the Frankish mayors of the palace.

In Francia during the 8th century, the mayors of the palace played a similar role as the modern-day British prime minister. Kings and queens still ostensibly ruled, but in matters of state and government, they were little more than figureheads. The real power belonged to the mayors, and the greatest mayor of them all was Charles Martel.

Battle of Tours, 732

Charles knew that the odds were stacked overwhelmingly against him.

The Frankish commander had arrayed his troops in a square formation around the wooded plain, across which a mountain wind swept with icy cold. He waited now, ready for an attack at any moment, and he was facing an enemy that had grown as quick as cancer—and twice as deadly.

Abd al-Rahman, also known as Abd er Rahman, the commander of the Muslim army that was rapidly bearing down upon Francia, was a formidable enemy. His cavalry was unlike anything that Western Europe had ever seen before. Swarthy men armed with bows and scimitars rode light-footed horses that never seemed to tire and moved with a speed and agility that the lumbering European cavalry could never hope to match. This combination was one that Europe found almost unbeatable, as that cavalry could mow down any army, and Charles knew that infantry units pitted against cavalry forces almost always ended in disaster. Yet here he was, ready to face Abd al-Rahman with a group of Frankish infantrymen. Greater armies than his had fallen and been destroyed at the blades of those Muslim horsemen.

The Umayyad Caliphate's roots went back almost exactly one hundred years. After the death of the Prophet Muhammad in 632, the Umayyad Caliphate emerged as the leading Muslim power, and its religious fervor drove its campaigns from continent to continent. North Africa and the Middle East didn't stand a chance. Now, the Umayyads had set their sights on Europe, and their conquest swept north and west like an uncontrollable flame. Already, the Duchy of Aquitaine, itself a part of Francia, had fallen to their trampling hordes.

Charles was the last line of defense to prevent the whole of Francia from falling to Abd al-Rahman. His group of infantrymen was the only thing that stood between Francia and the Umayyad Caliphate, and he knew that defeat would mean more than just the loss of land and life. It would mean the loss of Frankish culture. The Franks were still profoundly Catholic, while the Umayyads were profoundly Muslim. Not a soul in Francia would be left unaffected by the occupation of the Umayyads. Charles knew that he was standing at a crossroads in history itself. The stand he had taken near the city of Tours would send aftershocks through the centuries to come.

On October 10th, 732, Abd al-Rahman finally attacked. The vicious cavalry composed of Arabs and Berbers fell upon the Frankish infantry without mercy, and Charles's lines began to buckle. If the Battle of Tours had ended there, the same way that most of Abd al-Rahman's battles ended, then history itself would have quaked to its very foundations. The Umayyad soldiers would have crushed the Franks, the plain slick with mud and blood, and Abd al-Rahman would have pushed on unhindered to Paris itself.

It had happened over and over again in the past, but it did not happen on that day, for Charles struck at the Muslims again and again with a ferocity they had not grown to expect from the Europeans, a ferocity that earned the Frankish leader the name of Charles Martel: "Charles the Hammer." That hammer forged Europe on the anvil of the Umayyads that day, and incredibly, his infantry stood against Abd al-Rahman.

Meanwhile, behind enemy lines, Charles's scouts were heading fast to the Umayyad camp, which had been practically abandoned during the fighting. Frankish prisoners from Aquitaine were waiting there to be rescued, and the scouts made quick work of what guards were left, then set to freeing the prisoners. The camp was piled high with the bountiful spoils of the Muslims' conquests so far. Soon, word reached the battlefield that the camp was being robbed.

The Umayyad soldiers were hard pressed by Charles, and they were tired of fighting, as they were facing the very real possibility of defeat. When they heard that their booty was being carried off, they began to break ranks in a panic, rushing back to defend their camp. Chaos erupted throughout Abd al-Rahman's lines. Charles and his men pushed them harder, pressing home their newfound advantage, and somehow, incredibly, the Frankish infantry put all the Umayyads to flight. Those swift horses were sent bolting for home, many with empty saddles. Abd al-Rahman was pulled down and killed, and his army fell into chaos and fled.

Somehow, Charles Martel had turned the Battle of Tours into a victory, and it was a victory that would change global history forever. The man who fought it had already had plenty of experience in battle; in fact, he had paid for his title in blood.

Charles Martel

Charles was supposed to have inherited his title from his father, Pepin the Middle, who was the mayor of the palace before him. Charles considered the title to be rightfully his; he was, after all, Pepin's oldest son. Unfortunately, Charles Martel turned out to have the same enemy as Cinderella: a wicked stepmother. Plectrude, Pepin's second wife, sought to gain power for herself. She persuaded Pepin to disinherit Charles and make his grandson, Theudoald, his successor instead. Theudoald was a little boy at the time, while Charles was already well into his twenties and proving himself as a capable young man. Fearing that Charles and his supporters would overthrow her, Plectrude had the young man imprisoned after Pepin's death in 714.

Charles refused to languish in prison while Plectrude ruled as regent for his young nephew. Escaping from prison, Charles fled to another Frankish kingdom, Austrasia. Here, he found considerable support. The Austrasians considered him the rightful heir and were reluctant to be governed by a regency, so they provided him with the men and troops that he needed. Charles trained them personally, and after four long years of civil war and campaigning against Plectrude (as well as conquering Bavaria and Alemannia), he was finally able to claim his title of mayor of the palace.

His battle for the title provided him with invaluable experience, which would stand him in good stead when Abd al-Rahman arrived nearly twenty years later. His resounding victory against the Umayyads halted their progression into Europe, sending them back to the Middle East, a move that would change history forever. Yet that victory came at a high price.

One of the things that Charles had learned during his campaigns against his stepmother's forces was that conscripts were simply not good enough. Traditionally, during this feudal period, rulers would go to war primarily with fyrdmen—serfs that had received little training and possessed some rudimentary armor and weapons. These men were not career soldiers; they were farmers, and they spent more time tilling the land than training with their weapons. Charles had formed a standing army in Austrasia, a body of men dedicated to nothing but warfare, and it had proven to be the difference between victory and defeat. His was one of the few standing armies that the Umayyads would ever face in Europe, which may be why the Battle of Tours was a Frankish victory.

Standing armies, however, were rare for a reason. Serfs earned their own keep and went to battle for little or no pay, but soldiers needed to be fed, housed, and paid wages. In order to afford the army that had defeated the Umayyads, Charles had to resort to desperate measures. He began to seize large tracts of land that belonged to the Catholic Church, using them to generate income in the form of taxes, money that would have otherwise gone to the papacy. Even though Charles's conquest of the Umayyads may very well have saved the widespread occurrence of Catholic Christianity in that part of the world, the papacy was nonetheless deeply disgusted with him for taking their land. His actions caused a terrible rift between the rulers of Francia and the popes of Rome.

Nonetheless, Charles left behind a powerful legacy, and that legacy would only be expanded by his son and grandson who succeeded him.

Pepin the Short

As victorious as Charles was in warfare, he was unlucky in love. That's not to say that he had trouble finding a wife. After his sensational escape and flight to Austrasia, Charles married a girl there, Rotrude of Hesbaye. However, they enjoyed only six years of marriage together before Rotrude died. She left Charles with five children, including two sons. He named one Pepin after his father, while the other was called Carloman.

After Rotrude's death in 724, Charles headed off to campaign once again in Bavaria, where he came across another woman that could soothe his grieving heart. Her name was Swanahild, and she was nobly born, a fitting second wife for the most powerful man in Francia. She would bear him another son before his death, whose name was Grifo.

After the Battle of Tours, Charles would govern Francia for another nine years until his death in 741. He was around the age of 55 (his date of birth can only be guessed at). Instead of choosing a single heir from among his sons, Charles decided to divide the power between the two sons he had with Rotrude. He gave the larger lands of Neustria to Pepin, while Austrasia went to Carloman. Grifo was entirely left out, a fact that would soon lead to trouble for his two older half-brothers.

When he became mayor of the palace alongside Carloman, Pepin had already chosen a wife. Her name was Bertrada of Laon. Bertrada was a distant relation of Pepin's, and for that reason, their marriage was not sanctioned by the Church for several years. The Catholic Church was still against Charles Martel and his family thanks to the Hammer's treatment of Church lands, and the religious establishment sought any opportunity to bring disrepute to Charles's name, including their rejection of Pepin and Bertrada's marriage.

So, it came to be that, one year after Pepin became the mayor of the palace, Bertrada gave birth to a baby who would technically be born out of wedlock. The child was a strong and healthy son, and his parents named him after his grandfather. Perhaps they hoped that some of Charles Martel's greatness would rub off on little Charles. Little did they know that their son would grow up to become the greatest king that Francia had ever known.

* * * *

The boy would eventually be called Charlemagne, but as a child, he was known simply as Charles. Likely born in Aachen, Charles moved with his parents to the capital city of Paris soon after, where Pepin reigned and little Charles grew up. Not much is known of the boy's childhood. He was educated in the abbey of Saint-Denis by its abbot, who appears to have enjoyed teaching a student who was both enthusiastic and intelligent. As well as his native tongue, Charles learned both Latin and some Greek, and he could read and write as well. Literacy, at the time, was a privilege given only to the highborn and the rich—there had even been kings who could neither read nor write. Being literate in multiple languages was a noteworthy achievement in those days.

Being an only child at the time, Charles enjoyed having his mother's full attention lavished upon him. His father, however, was continually distracted. Pepin was fighting hard to defend his power.

Ever since Charles's father, Pepin the Short, and uncle, Carloman, had gained control over Francia, they had constantly been fighting to defend their power against their slighted half-brother. Backed by his mother's people, the Bavarians, Grifo was determined to grab what he believed to be his rightful share of Francian power.

For the first several years of Charles's life, his father was off campaigning against Grifo. Despite the fact that Pepin and Carloman had always had a tenuous relationship at best, they had no choice but to work together if they wanted to hold on to their own power. They finally succeeded in besieging Grifo's army and eventually pushed through his defenses to arrest him. Grifo was lucky that his half-brothers didn't kill him. Instead, he was forced to live out his days in a monastery, cut off from the outside world and incapable of holding any type of earthly power again.

Carloman would eventually share Grifo's fate. Slowly, Pepin began to pressure his brother, fighting for his vision of a unified Francia under a single ruler. It's unclear exactly why Carloman gave up his title and prestigious life. He may have done so voluntarily; it is also possible, however, that Pepin pressured Carloman into abandoning his title and becoming a monk himself in 747 when little Charles was only six years old. Carloman's power was left to Pepin, and thus, Charles's father became the sole ruler over all of Francia and one of the most powerful men in Europe.

However, before Carloman could join a monastery, he did make one very important political move. Mayors of the palace had the right to choose and appoint the kings of Francia from among the Merovingian family. Before his abdication, Carloman had chosen Childeric III, making him the figurehead king of the Frankish people. This move greatly chafed Pepin. He couldn't stand having any rivals to his power, not even one that had no real capacity to influence the government, and it seemed to him to be senseless to have a king who did nothing.

Pepin wanted Childeric gone. But many of the Franks were used to the idea of kings, and they'd never known a time when they were not governed by Merovingians. In order to get rid of Childeric, Pepin would need the backing of a strong ally. He could think of only one ally who had both the strength to bend the will of the Frankish people and the motivation to support a new Frankish king, and that was Roman Pope Zachary.

The papacy's soured relationship with the Merovingians—and, most recently, with Charles Martel—had cost it an important ally, one of the few powers in Western Europe that would have taken up arms to protect the pope. Large tracts of land belonged to the papacy in Italy, and the greedy surrounding kings were eyeing that land, hungering to add to their domains. Prominent among those were the kings of the Lombards, a Germanic tribe that had settled in Italy and established itself there as a powerful kingdom.

Pepin knew that Zachary was desperate—perhaps even desperate enough to form an alliance with the son of a man that the papacy fervently hated. He decided to reach out to Zachary in the form of a letter, which he dictated; Pepin, unlike Charles, was likely illiterate. He told Zachary that he considered it to be a grave injustice that a man with no real power should hold the title of king of the Franks, while the person who was doing all the heavy lifting would only be called the mayor of the palace. Pepin's intention was clear. He wanted to oust Childeric and make himself the king.

Zachary was delighted to receive Pepin's letter. He saw a wonderful opportunity to procure an ally who had proven himself in his war against Grifo and who commanded the army that had stopped even the Umayyads in their tracks. He swiftly responded, and soon, he found himself on his way to Paris.

In 751, Childeric III, the last of the Merovingians, was formally deposed. Zachary anointed Pepin as the king of the Franks—the first of a dynasty that would later be named the Carolingian dynasty, although it was not named after Pepin but after the ten-year-old boy who watched from the sidelines as his father's coronation took place. It must have been heady stuff for little Charles to watch the sparkling crown being placed upon his father's head, knowing that he was Pepin's eldest son. Someday, that crown would be his own. Perhaps at that moment, Charles knew, for the first time, the thrill of power.

Shortly after Pepin's coronation, Zachary returned to Rome and died there that same year. He was succeeded by Pope Stephen II.

Stephen, who had once been a Roman aristocrat, found himself in charge of a deeply threatened papacy. The Lombard king had captured the Exarchate of Ravenna shortly before Stephen became the pope, and it was obvious that the king was now setting his sights on Rome. Stephen turned tail and fled. He ran to the safest place he could think of: Paris. Pepin welcomed him with open arms, giving him sanctuary, and Stephen gratefully anointed him a second time in 753. The Lombard threat continued to grow, and Stephen begged Pepin to do something. As his power was firmly cemented in Francia itself, Pepin resolved to campaign against the Lombards.

Twelve-year-old Charles watched his father depart at the head of the great professional army that had beaten the Umayyads. This time, Charles was old enough to understand the risk that Pepin was taking. One can imagine that the sound of a marching army was one that the boy would never forget. And when Pepin returned soon afterward, with the Lombards soundly defeated and with Stephen installed once again in Rome, Charles's mind was made up. He, too, would be a glorious warrior one day. He wanted to win great battles, just like his father.

In gratitude for Pepin's actions, Stephen held another anointing ceremony for the Frankish king. This time, Charles and his brother Carloman (a toddler at the time) were anointed as well, as Pepin was eager for the boys to be established as the heirs to the Francian throne. Being anointed as the future king at the age of twelve must have been heady stuff for young Charles.

As for Pepin, he had not only defended Stephen's lands, but he had also expanded them into what would eventually become the Papal States. Stephen was eternally grateful, and Pepin's actions formed his most lasting legacy: the alliance between the Carolingian kings and Rome. Charles didn't know it yet, but Pepin's actions would someday change his life.

* * * *

By the time that Charles was a teenager, he had been joined by two more siblings. The first was a brother named Carloman, nine years Charles's junior. The second was a little sister called Gisela.

Charles and Carloman were trained in all the noble arts of young princes, considering that they were now heirs to a throne instead of just to a title. In fact, Charles may have had his first taste of battle around this time, as older teenage sons occasionally went to war with their fathers in this era. Pepin had been dealing with scattered rebellions all over his kingdom, especially from the particularly troublesome Duchy of Aquitaine, ever since he ascended to the throne, and in the latter part of his reign, these rebellions became more and more common.

Pepin was thoroughly engaged in keeping his own kingdom together when disaster struck once again for Rome. Stephen had died in 757, leaving his title to Pope Paul I. A new Lombard king, Desiderius, ascended to his throne at about the same time. Desiderius was an ambitious king and was determined to achieve what his predecessor had been unable to: rule over Rome. He began to march on the Papal States, and Pope Paul begged Pepin for help. But Charles's father was too busy fighting to keep his kingdom intact. He couldn't give aid to the papacy, no matter how much he wanted to.

This sorry state of affairs would continue for a full decade. As Pope Paul I watched in fear for the marching legions of Desiderius's army, Pepin struggled to contain the revolting Aquitanians, a battle that would eventually take him to his grave. In 768, the 54-year-old Pepin was on his way back to Paris after yet another campaign in Aquitaine when he died. It's unclear what exactly caused his death, but the most likely explanation is that he was mortally wounded in battle. He died at Saint-Denis, in Neustria, on September 24th, 768.

Charles was 26 years old when his father died, and Carloman was 17. Like his father before him, Pepin was reluctant to leave his kingdom to a single heir. Instead, he made Charles and Carloman the co-rulers of Francia. And it would soon become evident that—like their father and uncle—they had little desire to share the throne.

Chapter 3 – Sibling Rivalry

Without reliable sources to tell about Charles's and Carloman's childhood, we can only speculate on what their relationship was like as they grew up. In truth, they may not have had much of a relationship at all. The nine-year age gap between the two boys meant that they couldn't play together like most siblings do, which could have placed Carloman in the role of annoying tag-along little brother. However, it is more likely that they never really spent time with one another.

To make matters worse, it would appear that their personalities could not have been more different. Charles was vivacious, unstoppable, fiercely fearless, and impulsive. He dreamed of battles and kingdoms, of wars and splendor. On the other hand, Carloman was a quieter, more bookish type, a scholar and philosopher rather than a warrior prince. He was slow to act and quick to err on the side of peace, perhaps even verging on cowardice, especially in Charles's eyes.

Many may have considered Charles to be the kinglier of the two. He was, after all, the older brother; he had even been in a battle with Pepin on the campaign that claimed the old king's life. Yet perhaps Pepin viewed Charles as impulsive rather than decisive. Strangely, when Pepin divided his kingdom between his sons—who would reign as co-kings but hold their own lands and territories—he gave the majority of the land to Carloman. Charles had to make do with a far smaller share.

This chafed appallingly at Charles, and perhaps with good reason. He was 26 when his father died, making him far older, more experienced, and certainly much more able at defending the kingdom than Carloman. Charles had ridden out to war against Aquitaine. He had witnessed firsthand the gruesomeness of the battlefield, the cries of the dying, the blood running thick upon the Frankish earth. He must have felt that it was grossly unfair of Pepin—the father with whom Charles had stood shoulder to shoulder against their foes—to leave the majority of his lands and power to Carloman, who'd probably been safely sheltered in some fortress while this was happening.

Their relationship declined quickly and dramatically. In fact, hotheaded Charles may not have been far from marching his men on his own brother, thus plunging Francia into a harsh civil war, when something else drew his attention: the very same duchy whose rebellion had led to the death of his father.

The Rebellion of Aquitaine

Ever since the days of Charles Martel, Aquitaine had been a particularly troublesome duchy of Francia, as evidenced by Pepin's long and bloody struggle against them—a struggle that had eventually claimed his life. For eight long years, Pepin constantly fought against the duke of Aquitaine, Waiofar. Their bitter feud was horrifically destructive and not only on the battlefield. Surrounding peasants, farms, and peaceful little towns were all affected by the blight of war. It's possible that Charles had been by his father's side for every blow struck in the battle for supremacy. He was certainly a part of that last fateful campaign. It was in far-flung countries that Charles would someday claim his title of Charles the Great, but it was on the hills of Aquitaine that he was forged from an academic prince into a fine and furious warrior. His tall figure grew hard and lean, his hands dexterous with weapons, and his body flowed in unity with that of a powerful cavalry horse.

In the eighth year, with Charles still fighting alongside his father, the drawn-out struggle finally seemed to be drawing to a close. The people of Gascony, a nearby area and ally of Aquitaine, had fallen to Pepin in battle. Pepin's scorched-earth method of warfare destroyed countless towns, fortresses, and farms, leaving Waiofar without the resources to battle Pepin, who could draw on resources from the rest of his lands to fuel his armies. Waiofar himself remained ever elusive, never tasting the sharp edge of Charles's blade no matter how hard the warrior prince fought to bring him to bay. Eventually, it was his own men who turned against him. Some say that Pepin's messengers had turned Waiofar's own soldiers into assassins, perhaps promising them money in exchange for Waiofar's head. It's possible, though, that there were more insidious enemies—like fear, doubt, and hunger—responsible for the treachery of the Aquitanians. Either way, the war was practically over when they turned on Waiofar and killed him. Aquitaine and its allies surrendered, and Pepin rode home wounded but triumphant. He wouldn't live to enjoy his victory, dying on his way back to Paris.

As Charles arose to take the throne of the Franks, the Aquitanians realized that Pepin's death was an opportunity. Charles had not yet made himself so famous in battle as to frighten the Aquitanian lords; he was still a fledgling king, after all, youthful and inexperienced. Hastily, a kinsman of Waiofar—possibly his son—rose up to take the title of duke of Aquitaine. His name was Hunald II, and so, the conflict of two fathers became the conflict of two sons.

As soon as unrest began to rise again in Aquitaine in 769, just a year after Pepin had died, Charles was ready to leap into action. The blade of his sword was thirsty for vengeance. He was eager to put down the Aquitanians and avenge the death of Pepin, and he believed there was only one way to achieve his goal: war. After mustering the armies he had at his disposal, though, Charles realized that he didn't command the same fighting force that Pepin had. Most of Francia's armies were under Carloman's command. Much as Charles hated his brother, he needed him if he wanted to win this war, and so he was forced to humble himself and go to Carloman for assistance.

To his credit, Carloman did agree to meet with Charles. He left his home in Burgundy and brought some men down to an unspecified meeting place—possibly Paris—in order to discuss the matter of Aquitaine with his brother. Charles didn't want a discussion, though. He'd already made his decision: he was marching on Aquitaine, and Carloman was coming with him. But the eighteen-year-old king refused to be forced. He wanted nothing to do with the war that had taken their father, and, taking his armies with him, Carloman turned around and rode back to Burgundy.

Meanwhile, Hunald's strength was growing, and Charles's blood was up. Even though he had nowhere near the fighting force that he wanted, Charles refused to stand by and watch Hunald reclaim the lands that Pepin had fought so hard to protect. Perhaps it was because Carloman had not been in those battles that he did not understand the sacrifices that Pepin had made in order to gain some control over Aquitaine. But Charles had been there. And even if his brother refused to ride with him, he was going to war.

Advancing to Bordeaux, Charles established his men there, building a new fort at Fronsac. His army wasn't as large as he'd hoped it would be, but he was determined to beat the Aquitanians nonetheless.

Meanwhile, Hunald was not faring as well as he'd hoped either. Waiofar had not been defeated in one fell swoop. Instead, his numerous small allies—the Gascons, the people of Bourges, and others—had slowly crumbled away as Pepin beat away relentlessly at them. If Hunald was to hope to fight Charles, he would need allies. Sending his men out on guerrilla raids in a hopeless bid to hold off Charles's army, Hunald rode to Gascony looking for help. The

Gascons had assisted the Aquitanians in the past, and Hunald hoped they would fight together once more.

Unfortunately for Hunald, Duke Lupus II of Gascony was not so eager to make war with the Frankish king. When Hunald arrived at Lupus's court, help was not what he found. Instead, Lupus had him arrested, bound, and then dragged before King Charles.

Charles's campaign was over before it had truly begun. Pepin may have been the one who truly subdued Aquitaine and Gascony, but it was Charles who accepted their final surrender after years of fighting. Hunald was delivered at his very feet just as Syagrius had been delivered to Clovis: a helpless prisoner. Yet, strangely enough, Charles failed to execute Hunald as he might have done. Executions of enemy kings were commonplace at the time, but Charlemagne would use a different tactic. The age of chivalry was close at hand, and while few real men of the Middle Ages would live up to its legendary code, Charles, in this one instance, had mercy. He sent Hunald to live out his days in a monastery in peace, albeit robbed of all his ambitions.

Lupus, too, surrendered to Francia, and so, Charles won his first campaign without hardly striking a single blow. Aquitaine had fallen at last at the feet of Francia.

With the rebellion crushed, it was time for Charles to start looking to an area of kingship that perhaps did not appeal to his hot young blood the same way that war did: diplomacy. And in the Middle Ages, marriage was one of diplomacy's most important forms.

Charles's First Love – Or Was She?

The first romantic relationship recorded in Charles's life may not have been very romantic. In fact, it's likely that there was little real romance at all in the lives of the nobility at the time. Charles was never given the opportunity to choose his own wife or to marry for love. Instead, Pepin chose wives for both Carloman and Charles before his death.

Little is known about the women that Pepin had chosen to wed his sons, except that they were both Frankish and noble. He likely chose them from families that would strengthen the crown's political alliances. Either way, Charles and Carloman may have had little or no say in the matter, although it was likely none judging by how short-lived Charles's marriage was.

In fact, Charles's relationship with Himiltrude may not have even been a marriage at all. We're not sure that the Church ever truly sanctioned their union, but it's unclear why not. She might have been a concubine rather than a wife to Charles, or she could have been bound only by *Friedelehe*, a poorly understood Germanic relationship that seemed to have been some kind of betrothal or even a stand-in for a Church-approved marriage.

Either way, their relationship began in 768, the year that Pepin died, and she certainly looked fitting when she stood beside the tall and powerful Charles. War had hardened and tanned him, and despite his somewhat ungainly proportions, he was a sight to behold with his rich golden hair and powerful size. And according to his contemporaries, Himiltrude was splendid beside him. In fact, one writer described her as possessing "surpassing majesty" as she stood adorned with gold beside her royal lover.

Their relationship might have been loveless, but it was definitely not childless. While Charles was off fighting in Aquitaine, Himiltrude brought their first and only child into the world. The kings of the time customarily named their sons after their fathers, signifying that their sons were their heirs and would carry on their legacy. Just as Charles had been named after his grandfather, Charles Martel, he named his baby Pepin after his own father. Sadly, it would soon become apparent that the boy was badly deformed. He would later be known as Pepin the Hunchback.

While Charles may never have wed Himiltrude at all, Carloman wasted no time in marrying the bride Pepin had chosen for him, another Frankish noblewoman named Gerberga. Carloman likely married her in 768 as well when he was only seventeen. In the span of three years, they became parents to two sons, the eldest of whom was also named Pepin. Carloman may have been the quieter of the two brothers, but his choice of name for his son signified that he was by no means ready to surrender his crown. Instead, Carloman was convinced that young Pepin would someday be co-king alongside Charles's son of the same name.

Once again, after the Aquitanians were defeated and the two young princes were born, the kings may have come to blows if it hadn't been for a new diplomatic mission. And this one would change Charles's home life dramatically.

Desiderata, the Lombard Princess

In 756, the death of King Aistulf of the Lombards had precipitated chaos in the Lombard Kingdom. Aistulf's rule had been ambitious, as evidenced by his repeated bids to claim the papal lands, but when he died, he left his kingdom without a strong heir. The first claim to the throne would have lain with his brother, Ratchis. Ratchis, however, had moved to Monte Carlo and taken up a monk's habit. Accordingly, the dukes of the Lombard Kingdom all had their eyes on the throne.

It was the duke of modern-day Tuscany who moved most decisively. His name was Desiderius, and he amassed an army, setting his sights on the throne of the Lombards. With King Pepin the Short of the Franks still occupied with fighting the Aquitanians, there was nowhere for Pope Stephen II to run, and he could only watch in horror as civil war loomed among the Lombards.

But Desiderius had other foes to deal with. In the face of Aistulf's death, Ratchis did the unthinkable: he revoked his vows and announced his own claim to the throne. His leap from monk to king was viewed as a terrible sin by the Catholic Church, in whose eyes the monastic vows were meant to be lifelong.

As Italy teetered on the brink of civil war, Desiderius realized that he and Pope Paul I (Stephen's successor in 757) had a common enemy: Ratchis. Ratchis wanted the same throne that Desiderius did, and he had spurned the Church that Paul now stood for. Setting aside his ambitions for the Papal States for now, Desiderius turned to the pope and offered him a truce—and a deal. He would surrender some Lombard towns to the pope's control if Paul would offer Desiderius his support and acknowledge him as the king of the Lombards. Ready to get his revenge on Ratchis, Paul was quick to accept Desiderius's offer. An uneasy peace was forged between the papacy and the Lombards, and Ratchis wisely decided to flee, leaving the throne open for Desiderius, who quickly seized power and became the king.

The relationship between the papacy and the Lombards, unfortunately, would not remain so stable. Desiderius never lost his thirst for the Papal States, and with no other major enemies to occupy him, Pope Paul I was well aware that the Lombard king could invade at any moment. Unfortunately for Paul, his only real ally, Pepin, would spend the rest of his reign embroiled in the conflict with Aquitaine. After Paul's death in 767, Desiderius went as far as to interfere with the papal succession, crowning a pope of his own choosing, who reigned only briefly before he was rejected by the Romans.

It was only when Charles took the throne, and Aquitaine had finally been subdued, that the new pope, also named Stephen, began to see a glimmer of hope against Rome's old foe. This time, however, help from Francia did not come in the form of armored knights riding in to rescue Stephen III. It came instead in the form of diplomacy, and it was not Charles who brought the diplomatic mission to Italy but his mother, Bertrada.

It's unclear who exactly initiated the negotiations of peace between the Franks and the Lombards, Desiderius or Bertrada. Both had valid reasons for seeking something more solid than the unhappy truce between the Lombards and the papacy. Desiderius had no desire to make an enemy of Francia, as that had been Aistulf's fatal mistake. And Bertrada, impressed though she must have been by Charles's conquest in Aquitaine, was well aware that her son was no match for Desiderius just yet. He had only been king for two years, after all, and the rebellion in Aquitaine had already been all but crushed when he took the throne.

So it was that the queen mother of the Franks and the king of the Lombards came together in peace, and they solidified that peace in the most medieval way possible: by marriage. Desiderius had fathered at least four lovely daughters, and he chose one of them to be sent to Francia to marry a man who had been the enemy of her people. Her name is somewhat disputed. History knows her well as Desiderata, which may not be accurate; some sources suggest that "Desiderata" was recorded in error and actually referred to Desiderius himself and that her real name was Gerperga. This name, however, may have arisen through confusion between Charles's wife and Carloman's wife, who was named Gerberga.

Either way, the Lombard princess was likely little more than a teenager when she found herself being sent across the mountains with the Frankish queen mother to be united in marriage to an unknown king. One can only speculate how frightened the girl must have been as she traveled to Francia. She must have heard the stories of how Pepin had put the Lombards to flight and butchered her own people, and now, she had no choice but to marry his son.

The pope was no more pleased with the marriage than Desiderata was. He had hoped that Charles would come charging gloriously over the mountains and defeat the Lombards in battle, not marry one of their princesses. However, there was little that he could do to stop the wedding from happening, and so, King Charles of Francia married Princess Desiderata of the Lombards in 770. To do so, he had to put Himiltrude aside.

It's difficult to ascertain what Charles's marriage to Desiderata was really like. There are no real records of the personal nature of their relationship, yet it's no leap of the imagination to think that there couldn't have been much love between them. Desiderata could have done worse than Charles—at least he was young and handsome—but both of them had still been forced into marriage likely against their will. It's possible that neither had seen the other before their wedding day, and Charles would probably have been much happier to ride into Italy and subdue the Lombards with the edge of the sword rather than marry into their family.

Either way, there appears to have been little intimacy between them. In their one year of marriage, Desiderata would bear no children.

The Brink of War

It's easy to speculate that Charles's loss of Himiltrude and his marriage to Desiderata did little other than to fuel his hatred for Carloman. Carloman was married with two healthy sons and was still in control of most of Francia, despite the fact that it was Charles who had had to fight the Aquitanians alone, Charles whose child was born with a deformity, and Charles who'd been forced to put aside his wife and marry a Lombard princess.

By 770, Charles and Carloman's relationship had soured dramatically. Once again, civil war loomed. With the rebellion crushed and the Lombards dealt with, Charles had no one to fight except his brother. It's possible that Francia might have descended into civil war or that Carloman would have suffered the same destiny as his ill-fated uncle of the same name: being quietly forced into life as a monk.

But before any of this could come to pass, tragedy struck Carloman and his small family in 771. Despite being only twenty years old, Carloman died out of the blue. By all accounts, his death came about as the result of natural causes, perhaps a catastrophic hemorrhage. He left Gerberga and their two sons behind, as well as an empty throne.

The vacuum left by Carloman's death was one that Charles was only too eager to fill, even though it was not rightfully his. In the years that followed, the fight for Carloman's throne would swallow up several nations into its sour belly—and it would begin to pave the way for Charles's rise from co-king of Francia to Holy Roman emperor.

Chapter 4 – To the Pope's Rescue

Illustration II: A 15ᵗʰ-century depiction of Charlemagne and Pope Adrian I.

The tragic early death of Carloman would shake the foundations of several countries, France and Italy among them. Yet no one was as unexpectedly and harshly affected as Gerberga and her two little boys.

Like everyone else, Gerberga hadn't expected Carloman to die so soon, and his death shattered her world. Whatever her feelings had been for her husband, he had provided her with protection and stability in a world where noblewomen and their children could easily become targets. She knew that Charles hated Carloman, but the latter had held enough power that Charles hesitated to attack him outright. Now, Carloman was dead, and Gerberga's protection against Charles was gone.

If it hadn't been for Charles, Gerberga's life might not have changed much after Carloman's death. She would have become a regent for her son Pepin, who would have taken his rightful place as king in due time when he was old enough. In the meantime, Gerberga would have been one of the most powerful women in the known world. But she knew that Charles would have no respect for the rightful succession of his brother's throne. She wasn't sure what he would do to her or to her two toddlers (the eldest of whom was only three years old), but she knew that it wouldn't be good. She had to get away from Francia if she wanted her son to be king—or even to survive at all.

As Charles was hugely popular in Francia itself, Gerberga knew that it would be no use at all to attempt to find sanctuary in her home country. Instead, she could think of only one ally strong enough to protect her and her boys from Charles: Desiderius, the king of the Lombards. His truce with Charles, despite Bertrada's best efforts, had been short-lived. A few months before Carloman died, Charles had rejected Desiderius and his people on every conceivable level, as he had divorced the Lombard princess.

Divorcing Desiderata

Divorce, as we know it today, did not exist in the Middle Ages. The concept of simply ending a marriage was utterly unthinkable at the time; marriage vows were truly binding for life. And while lower-born people, such as serfs and peasants, could escape the notice of the Church and simply abandon their spouses, the nobility did not have that choice.

There was no legal way to actually end a marriage in Charles's time, no matter how intolerable it may have felt. However, a marriage could be terminated if it could be proven that it had never been valid in the first place. This process, called annulment, was the only way that noble-born people could escape from a union that they could no longer bear. There were a variety of reasons why marriages could be annulled, including infidelity, marriage under false pretenses, or consanguinity—being too closely related. This was a particular favorite of nobility at the time since most nobles were related to each other somehow, and the Church officially disallowed marriages between people who shared any ancestors in seven generations.

Another reason for annulment, however, was infertility. This may sound strange, but in an era where producing a viable heir could mean the difference between decades of peace and years of turmoil for an entire country, fertility was vitally important in noble marriages. Birthing an heir was a massive part of every queen's responsibility. And here is where Desiderius's daughter appears to have failed Charles.

After a year of marriage, Desiderata had still failed to give birth to an heir for Charles, and he turned to Pope Stephen III, asking for the marriage to be annulled. Stephen was very ill at the time, but he was more than happy to destroy the alliance between the Franks and the Lombards, as it was an alliance he had never approved of, one that could have meant disaster if the Lombards ever decided to invade Rome as Desiderius often threatened to do. He briskly annulled the marriage, and Desiderata was sent back to Italy, a rejected queen, forced out of the title she'd never asked for.

It's hard to say exactly why Charles really wanted to end his marriage to Desiderata. He did have a valid reason to be concerned about his lack of an heir; with Carloman's two boys as healthy as ever, Charles was feeling pressured to have a son of his own who would be a more capable king than Pepin the Hunchback. However, poor Desiderata had hardly been given a chance to prove herself as a fertile queen, having been married to Charles for only a year.

Another possibility was that Charles had found a different woman and realized that marrying her would be a much smarter move politically than staying with Desiderata. This seems likely, as he had hardly sent Desiderata way from him before he was standing in a wedding ceremony. Her name was Hildegard of the Vinzgau, and she was only about thirteen years old at the time. However, marrying her would win Charles an ally he desperately wanted. Hildegard's father was a powerful count who owned a vast amount of land within Carloman's part of Francia. He would have been a dangerous enemy if he had allied with Carloman, but when Charles married Hildegard, he turned the count into a useful friend. Perhaps divorcing Desiderata was done explicitly in order to marry Hildegard and build an alliance that could help Charles if he decided to make war on Carloman after all.

One can easily speculate that Charles truly could not tolerate living with Desiderata. Marrying her had hardly been his own idea after all. Perhaps their relationship had simply devolved to such a disgusting point that Charles could no longer stand it and would do anything to escape from their relationship, even to the point of damaging his truce with Desiderius.

On the other hand, it's entirely possible that breaking the peace with the Lombard Kingdom was exactly what Charles had wanted. Charles was hungry to expand his power. He had already conquered Pepin's old enemies, the Aquitanians; he may have been spoiling to do the same to the Lombards.

Either way, divorcing Desiderata was a disgusting insult to Desiderius, destroying what little friendliness there had been between the Franks and the Lombards. The atmosphere was as ripe for war as dry undergrowth for a wildfire. All that it needed to ignite was one small spark—and that spark came with the death of Carloman on December 4th, 771.

War Begins with the Lombards

Gerberga's flight to the Lombard capital of Pavia could not have been an easy one. There were only two ways for her to reach Italy in safety: either by sea or by land. The sea routes were treacherous at best, made almost impassable in winter; the mountain passes would have been similarly perilous in midwinter. She could not have hoped to cross the mountains by carriage. Instead, she would have had to ride, with her one- and three-year-old sons too young to control their own ponies.

It's difficult to imagine how hard this journey must have been for Gerberga. For starters, she was little more than a child herself; if she had wed at thirteen, the traditional age for princesses, she would have been only seventeen or eighteen at this point. Winter was cruel, and the road was long. It would have been a grueling trek across a frigid, friendless landscape for this young mother and her little boys.

Yet somehow, Gerberga managed to reach the court of Desiderius, where she was welcomed with caution. Desiderius knew her as the sister-in-law of his chief enemy now that Charlemagne had rejected Desiderata, but he could also see an opportunity in her desperation. When Gerberga begged him for protection, Desiderius realized that he could provide much more. In fact, if he could, he would try to make her two sons the kings of Francia. He recognized the fact that Charles was a dangerous enemy. He also realized that having a client king of his on the throne of Francia would give him an important ally on the very doorstep of his enemy. If he could get little Pepin onto the throne of Francia, he could be Pepin's regent, controlling a large part of Charles's country. Or, even better, Charles would be engaged in a civil war in his own land and leave the Lombard Kingdom alone.

For Pepin to be made king, however, the papacy would have to be on board with Desiderius's plans. And Desiderius's relationship with the papacy had done nothing but decline since he meddled with their affairs after Paul's death in 767. Stephen III viewed Desiderius as a grave enemy. Yet the Lombard king was as wily as he was powerful, and even though he hadn't been able to determine the next pope, he still had friends in Rome. Stephen III was sickly and uninvolved, and Desiderius hoped that perhaps one of his Roman sympathizers would be able to overrule the pope and show the Lombards some support. His ultimate goal was for Carloman's sons to be anointed as kings, just as Carloman himself, as well as Charles, had been back when Pepin had first put the Lombards to flight in the 750s.

His plan might just have worked if not for another ill-timed death that would ultimately doom Desiderius and all of his schemes. In 772, shortly after Gerberga arrived at Pavia with her children, Pope Stephen III died. Desiderius scrambled to try to intervene in the papal succession once more; however, he was unsuccessful, and to his horror, Stephen was replaced by Pope Adrian I. Adrian was as anti-Lombard as it was possible to be, and he had no love for Desiderius.

Desiderius quickly had to abandon any hope of getting Pepin and his little brother anointed. Instead, he left his schemes of seizing Frankish land behind and focused on protecting his own. Back in 757, when Desiderius had first become the king of the Lombards, he had done so by bargaining with the pope of the time, offering to surrender certain cities to him in exchange for papal support against Ratchis. Conniving as he was, Desiderius had never actually surrendered those cities to Rome, a fact that Stephen had conveniently ignored. Adrian, on the other hand, did not plan on turning a blind eye. He confronted Desiderius, demanding that the Lombard king keep his word and give up several cities in Ravenna to papal control.

Desiderius would not be so easily cowed. He had never given in to the popes' demands before. Surely, he could conquer Adrian just as he'd conquered the popes before him. Desiderius immediately refused to surrender the cities; instead, he decided that it was high time to launch the invasion he'd been threatening to begin for decades. He attacked the Papal States themselves, and Adrian found himself cornered just as Stephen II had been in the time of Aistulf.

At first, Adrian was determined to handle Desiderius on his own. He was the pope, after all—one of the most powerful men in Europe— and he was sure he could protect his lands and people against some petty Lombard king. But it quickly became evident that Adrian's armies were no match for Desiderius. As he faced the very real threat of losing Rome entirely to the invading king, Adrian realized that he had no choice. After holding out against Desiderius for several months, he began to look for an ally to turn to. And like the popes before him, Adrian would see that his only hope was the king of the Franks.

In 773, word reached King Charles from Rome, and he met with Roman ambassadors at Thionville. At the time, he had just returned from his first hard war with the Saxons (which will be explored in a later chapter). The war had shown that he was not only a battle-hardened warrior, who was capable of suppressing revolts in his own realm, but that he also was a king who could subdue entire nations. What was more, he had just repudiated Desiderata, so his relationship with Desiderius was clearly no longer a friendly one.

Even though Adrian hadn't had much communication with Charles yet, he suspected that the young king might prove to be a strong ally for the Church. Charles had not only conquered the Saxons, but he had also Christianized them, sometimes brutally. Whether or not he actually followed the values of the Church was one thing, but it was clear that his political alliance lay with the Catholic Church.

For those reasons, it was little surprise, although it must have been of great relief to Adrian, that Charles responded swiftly, ready to fulfill his role as the protector of Rome, despite the fact that Desiderius's own ambassadors had also traveled to Thionville to meet with him. Charles was no friend of Desiderius. Still, his appetite for war had been tempered by experience, and he hoped he would be able to cool Desiderius's temper without violence. There was little hope of solving their problems with diplomacy, so Charles decided to try bribery instead. He offered Desiderius a bribe of an unknown amount of gold in exchange for the cities that Adrian demanded.

Desiderius, however, would not be cowed by a young Frankish king. He had a trump card up his sleeve: Gerberga and her sons. If he could beat Charles in battle and force Adrian to anoint Carloman's son Pepin as king, he could put a client king on the throne of Francia. Desiderius was ready for war, and Charles's earlier reluctance vanished. There was nothing else to do besides to march an army over the Alps and meet Desiderius in battle.

The Siege of Pavia

As the winter of 773 approached, Charles gathered his powerful standing army and approached the Alps. He was aided by a strong and experienced commander: his uncle Bernard, a son of Charles Martel himself. It wasn't long before their invasion was met with strenuous resistance. At the very feet of the Italian Alps, Desiderius had set his army in array, ready to do battle with the Franks.

Charles had grown wiser during his battles with the Saxons. Instead of marching directly on Desiderius as he had done with the Aquitanians, the young king started to look for a weakness. He would find the same weakness as one of the first Frankish kings did hundreds of years before when meeting with the intimidating Attila the Hun: Desiderius had failed to protect his flanks. A sneak attack on the flanks of the army could prove devastating, and so, Charles and Bernard split up and sneaked down through the frosted mountainside, then pinched Desiderius's army between the two of them and fell upon the Lombard flanks with unexpected savagery.

The battle was brief. The Lombard army was devastated, scattered across the snow by Charles's powerful army, and Desiderius had no choice but to flee. His border shattered, he realized that his only hope was to protect his capital, Pavia.

Founded in 220 BCE as a Roman settlement, then named Ticinum, Pavia was already more than five centuries old by the time

Desiderius rode back to it with his tail between his legs. It had already had a long history haunted by ignominy. Always a powerful city in Italy, it had even been the seat of Romulus Augustus, the last emperor of the old Western Roman Empire. He had been defeated there in 476 CE, and now, Desiderius had to face the grim reality that his fate could be very much the same. The last emperor of Rome had sought safety at Pavia, and the last king of the Lombards now did the same.

Withdrawing his army and people into Pavia, Desiderius locked its great gates and dug in, preparing for the siege that was now inevitable. Charles and Bernard marched up to the city and took their time in laying a siege. There was no need for them to catapult great rocks into the walls or mount ladders and grappling hooks up to its towering battlements; they had a far greater weapon than that: starvation. Simply by preventing anyone from leaving the city, the Franks could secure their victory.

Well, almost anyone. One Lombard did escape the beleaguered capital, and it was Adelchis, the single son of King Desiderius and the one-time brother-in-law of Charles. He fled Pavia as fast as he could ride, not simply for cowardly reasons. Instead, he had an important mission: he had to protect the one great asset that could be Desiderius's last hope, Carloman's family. Gerberga and her two sons were holed up in Verona, a hundred miles away from the siege.

Upon reaching Verona, Adelchis realized that the Lombards' situation was utterly dire. They were surrounded by powerful Franks, and Charles had proven to be more than a match for Desiderius. If Adelchis was going to find a way to beat his ex-brother-in-law, he was going to need more than just the late Carloman's son and apparent rightful heir to the throne of Francia. He'd need a powerful ally, one that could face both the Franks and the Romans.

The most obvious choice was an old enemy of Rome, the Byzantine, or Eastern Roman, Empire. While its split from the ancient Western Roman Empire in 285 CE was peaceful, a decision made by Emperor Diocletian when he realized that the Roman

Empire as a whole was too large for one emperor to administrate, the split had proven to open a great rift between the two halves. Everything about the Byzantine Empire was different from their Roman counterparts, not least their religion, as they were Eastern Orthodox Christians instead of Roman Catholics. The Byzantine emperor would have no qualms about facing the Roman pope.

But Adelchis's efforts proved to be too little, too late. Even as he begged the Byzantines for help and struggled to scrape together an army of his own, Adelchis's enemy was hot on his trail. Leaving the capable Bernard in charge of the siege at Pavia, Charles rode after the young prince, determined to stamp out every last hope that Desiderius had. Verona fell quickly before Charles's onslaught. Adelchis once more abandoned the conquered city, fleeing to Constantinople, and Carloman's little family was left without any protection from their vengeful uncle.

It would appear, however, that Charles stripped them of their titles yet spared their lives. It's uncertain exactly what happened to Gerberga and her two little boys, but there is no record of their deaths. As was Charles's habit, they were likely forced to join an abbey and live out their lives in quiet anonymity, even though the blood of princes and kings flowed in their veins.

With the sons of both Carloman and Desiderius dealt with, Charles returned to Pavia, which was still under siege. It would remain that way for around ten months. There was no need for dramatic battles this time. Charles and Bernard waited calmly for starvation to do its work. In fact, Charles himself didn't spend all his time at Pavia either. He journeyed three hundred miles to celebrate Easter in Rome in the spring of 774, where he was gratefully received by Adrian.

As summer came in green abundance to the foothills of the Alps, the citizens of Pavia failed to experience nature's beauty and bounty. Instead, they were starving. Desiderius could watch them die no longer. He had no choice but to surrender, and Charles triumphantly plucked the crown from the emaciated Lombard king. Desiderius may have expected that he would be forced to pay tribute to Charles or rule underneath him, but Charles was not content with simply forcing Desiderius into submission. Instead, he wanted Desiderius's titles for his own. The last king of the Lombards was cloistered and stripped of his titles, and Charles had himself crowned as the king of the Franks and Lombards. It was around this time that people first began to call him Charles the Great or Carolus Magnus, a name that would eventually be shortened into its modern-day version of Charlemagne.

The remaining Lombards were divided on what they could do now that Charlemagne was ruling over them. Some dukes wisely allied themselves with Charlemagne and lived peacefully under his reign; others couldn't face life under the Franks and fled over the mountains to modern-day Genoa. Still others, however, waited in the hopes that Adelchis would return from Constantinople. The young man was treated well there and eventually did get the military support he'd wanted. Years later, in 787, Byzantine Empress Irene would attempt to cultivate an alliance between the Byzantines and Charlemagne by soliciting his daughter's hand in marriage to her son. When her offer was rejected, she gave Adelchis an army and sent him off to attack Italy.

Adelchis returned at last to be the new hope for his people, but their hope would turn out to be false. The Lombard duke of Benevento, Grimoald III, had been more or less forced to fight on Charlemagne's side, and together with the Frankish forces, he soundly defeated Adelchis. The Lombard prince's campaign was over before it had even started, as he fought only one battle that was such a resounding defeat that it brought about an official end to the Lombard Kingdom forever. It rallied briefly a few years later when Grimoald himself attempted to throw off the Frankish shackles that bound him, but Charlemagne's sons quickly defeated him.

As for Adelchis, no one knows his ultimate fate. He may have died on the battlefield or fled once again to live out his days in Constantinople, a failed hero without any titles.

Chapter 5 – The One Defeat

Conquering the Lombard Kingdom placed Charlemagne in charge of one of the largest kingdoms in Europe. He had established himself already as a force to be reckoned with, but his appetite for expansion was never satiated. In fact, it only grew, and with everything peaceful on the Italian front, Charlemagne was seeking a new direction in which to expand. He was already involved in the Saxon Wars in the east; now, he turned his eyes to the south. And this tumultuous part of Europe was ripe for conquest.

The State of the South

Ever since his first conquest in 769, the thoroughly subdued people of Aquitaine had been meek and biddable. This was helped by the fact that Charlemagne appointed several of his most powerful allies as dukes over the surrounding areas, such as Toulouse and Bordeaux. But while Aquitaine was behaving itself nicely, Gascony was quite another affair.

Lupus II, the duke who had so willingly betrayed Hunald, which had led to the conquest of Aquitaine in 769, had quickly submitted to Charlemagne. Now, however, he had grown tired of submitting to marauding Franks. He would not go belly up again so easily.

While Gascony officially belonged to Francia, the reality was very different. Its people—largely members of the Basques—saw themselves as independent warriors who would not be so easily shunted around by some Frankish king. The Basques were an ancient people. They endure to this day as a unique ethnic group, with mysterious origins and a culture that grew in almost complete isolation, leading to enormous distinctions from their surrounding peoples. Everything from their language to their DNA is unrelated to the surrounding tribes.

The Basques were a proud, independent, pagan race in the late 8th century, and Charlemagne, with his orderly empire and Christianization policies, was determined to change that. He was eager to suppress them, trampling them down into an easy highway all the way to the Pyrenees, which formed the southern border of France with Spain. If he could cross the Pyrenees, he stood to invade the lands that lay even farther south. And these were particularly appealing to Charlemagne as they were ruled by some of the greatest enemies of the Roman Catholic Church: the Muslims.

Ever since Charles Martel had faced the Umayyad Caliphate on the battlefield of Tours nearly fifty years before, Muslims and Christians had been locked in a continuing battle. Charles Martel had succeeded in driving them back out of France, but they were still in control of almost the entire Iberian Peninsula. However, these Muslims were not all members of the Umayyad Caliphate. Instead, many of them were Abbasids, and they were no friends of the Umayyads.

The governor of Hispania—modern-day Spain, including some other territories on the Iberian Peninsula—was Sulayman al-Arabi, an Abbasid. He was feeling increasingly threatened by the emir of Cordoba, an Umayyad, and he knew that he needed to find a way to keep his lands under his possession before the sweeping Umayyad hordes took over. Forming an alliance with two other powerful Abbasids—Abu Taur of Huesca and Husayn of Zaragoza—he agreed with them that they needed to seek an alliance with another power. Any power, so long as it would stand against the Umayyads.

As surprised as Charles must have been to receive Muslim ambassadors, he was eager to find out more when he realized that they were seeking a military alliance. Fighting alongside the Abbasids could provide the perfect opportunity to crush Gascony. What was more, Charles was seeking to expand into Hispania itself, driving back the Muslims, starting with the Umayyads, and growing an ever-greater Roman Catholic empire.

In 778, Charles decided to accept al-Arabi's offer of alliance. He knew that he would be facing his most formidable enemy to date if he marched on the Muslims, and so, he mustered the biggest army he could. Pulling every spare man into the massive ranks of his power, he marched at last over the Pyrenees. Sending one half of his army over the eastern part of the mountains and leading the rest over the western part, he crossed through the passes without mishap, soon arriving in Hispania to a warm welcome from al-Arabi.

Al-Arabi was ready to do battle at once. Their first target was Zaragoza. While its leader, Husayn, ostensibly was an ally of al-Arabi's, Charlemagne's enemy had beaten him to the city. The Umayyad Caliphate had sent one of its most important generals to secure Zaragoza: Thalaba Ibn Obeid. But it would seem that Ibn Obeid had underestimated Husayn's power. For whatever reason, he was unable to subdue Zaragoza, and Husayn clapped him in irons and imprisoned him.

Charlemagne and al-Arabi likely didn't know this, though. They marched on Zaragoza to liberate it from the Umayyads only to find it firmly under the control of Husayn, whose ego had become rather inflated by his recent capture of Ibn Obeid. Having conquered the Umayyads all by himself, Husayn decided that he didn't need help, especially not from some Christian Frankish king with an ulterior motive. He refused to allow Charlemagne and al-Arabi entrance into the city.

Charlemagne was enraged. Al-Arabi had promised him that controlling Zaragoza would be a walk in the park thanks to Husayn's involvement, and now, he'd been betrayed by his new allies. Deciding he'd been wrong to ally himself with the Abbasids after all, Charlemagne arrested al-Arabi and laid siege to Zaragoza.

The siege, however, was short-lived. Husayn was stubborn, and Charlemagne had begun to realize that capturing Hispania with its messy politics wasn't going to be as easy as he had first assumed. After a month's siege, he reached a truce with Husayn, agreeing to leave the city alone in exchange for certain prisoners and a rather substantial amount of gold and treasure. Husayn gratefully accepted, and Charlemagne turned around, setting his sights on his real target: Gascony.

With al-Arabi still in chains with his army, Charlemagne set about subduing the Basques who lived on both sides of the Pyrenees. His goal was not so much to capture the territories—officially, they belonged to him already—as it was to simply break the spirits of the Basque people. His soldiers were permitted to do as they pleased, and they pleased to destroy everything. They crashed into towns full of innocent people, setting houses and farms alight, driving women and children through the streets, razing entire villages to the ground. Homes, lives, and businesses were taken, destroyed, and left as scattered ashes and black scars of charred earth.

The remaining Basques were relentlessly oppressed, abused in every way by Charlemagne and his soldiers. They were hopelessly mistreated, and to add insult to injury, Charlemagne did not spare their capital, Pamplona. He did not destroy this city; after all, it was important to an economy that now had to pay him tribute. Instead, he simply stripped away its defenses, laying it bare and vulnerable to any form of invasion. He had its walls—the pride and protection of any medieval city—pulled down. Pamplona was left as naked and beaten as a peasant in the stocks.

This would prove to be a fatal mistake. Pulling down Pamplona's walls had been easy, but breaking the spirit of its people would turn out to be all but impossible. Instead of growing submissive, the Basques became bitter and angry. Their duke was determined not to give in the way he'd done nearly a decade before. And while the Basques could not hope to meet Charlemagne in a pitched battle, there was another way that they could get back at him for all he had done to their people.

Their plans were enabled at last when they received help from a fellow enemy of Charlemagne, the family of Sulayman al-Arabi. He was still being dragged around with Charlemagne's army, a prize prisoner, like some captive wild animal for the masses to gawk at. They were determined to get him back, and the Basques were more than ready to help.

So, even as Charlemagne plundered and pillaged wherever he would, his one and only downfall was being plotted in the mountainsides of the Pyrenees.

The Battle of Roncevaux Pass

By the warm summer of August 778, Charlemagne decided that his southern campaign was over. He may not have won Zaragoza as he'd hoped, but the Basques had been thoroughly defeated, and the governor of Hispania was with him in chains. Saxony was calling him west for further warfare, and he would later return to conquer Hispania. It was time for him to go home.

Charlemagne began to lead his vast, bloated army back over the Pyrenees, this time keeping them all together in one trampling, destructive mass of men and horses. The baggage train, in particular, was grossly swollen with prisoners and plunder. Huge amounts of treasure had been laden into carts drawn by beasts of burden. Charlemagne's army was a mighty one, but it was also massive and slow, and it crawled across the mountains under the heaviness of its power.

The Basques, on the other hand, were as quick as mountain goats on the rocky passes. Armed with spears and going on foot, they knew the landscape better than anyone, melting in and out of the mountains like wild animals. They knew that the perfect place for an ambush was the narrow Roncevaux Pass. Arraying themselves among the rocks and foliage, armed to the teeth and ready for vengeance, aided by Al-Arabi's family, the Basques waited.

Oblivious of the little army hidden in the rocks mere yards from them, Charlemagne's soldiers marched merrily through the pass, grown perhaps a little careless from the easy and wanton destruction they'd wrought on the Basques. The bloated baggage train trailed along behind, weighed down with treasure, prisoners, and provisions for the soldiers. Surrounding and following the baggage train was the rearguard, a considerable force of some of Charlemagne's best men who brought up the rear of the army and protected the baggage train. Charlemagne's rearguard was commanded by several of his most high-ranking officers, including Roland, the military governor of the Breton March. Charlemagne was confident that they would be able to protect his army against some unforeseen rear attack.

His confidence was misplaced, not so much because of the competence of the commanders but because of the unexpected savagery with which the Basques and their allies would fall upon him.

Hidden in the surroundings of Roncevaux Pass, the Basques and Abbasids waited, biding their time until the great mass of Charlemagne's army had passed by. When only the baggage train and the rearguard were in sight, they launched their attack in their unseen hundreds.

The first that the Frankish commanders knew of the ambush was the sound of javelins and arrows hissing through the air, then the deadly slap as sharp projectiles met human flesh. As screams rang out, the Frankish commanders frantically searched for an invisible enemy. They never had the time to organize any real defense. By the time the Franks realized that Basque and Abbasid soldiers were attacking them, their enemies were already pouring down from the mountainside, armed with spears, knives, and short swords. Charlemagne's men were surrounded in moments; the fighting was quick, brutal, and significantly one-sided. All of the training Charlemagne's commanders received, many of whom would have been raised with warfare in mind, proved to be no match for the surprise attack that now faced them. They began to die quickly.

The Battle of Roncevaux Pass was not so much a fight as it was a slaughter. The Frankish soldiers never really stood a chance, not against such a well-planned ambush driven by such a burning desire for revenge against all the evils Charlemagne and his men had committed against the Basque people. Every single member of the Frankish rearguard was killed. The rest of Charlemagne's army escaped relatively unscathed; the rearguard sacrificed itself in slowing down the Basques and Abbasids long enough for Charlemagne to get the rest of his men out of the pass and onto open ground, where no one would dare to face him in a pitched battle.

It was still a crushing defeat for the Franks. Even though the rearguard was a comparatively small part of Charlemagne's army, it had included some of his very best commanders, and there was some turmoil in Francia due to the death of so many high-ranking men. To add insult to injury, all of the treasure that Charlemagne had accumulated in that campaign—including the gold that Husayn had paid him to leave Zaragoza alone—had been carried off by the Basques. Perhaps worst of all, Sulayman al-Arabi had gone free. His children had rescued him, and so, Charlemagne ended up not conquering the Abbasid rulers of Hispania, instead making a great enemy out of them. Sulayman al-Arabi himself, however, would not live long enough to be an enemy of Charlemagne. He was killed just two years later by the ever-treacherous Husayn of Zaragoza.

The Battle of Roncevaux Pass would go down in history as the only major defeat that Charlemagne would ever suffer. It was a tragedy in its time for the Franks, especially for Charlemagne, but throughout

the rest of his long and warlike rule, Roncevaux Pass would be the only time he drank of the bitter draft of defeat. While not all of his battles would end in decisive victories, never again would he taste of it.

Unfortunately, while Charlemagne may have learned something from Roncevaux, he certainly did not learn how to treat his subjects better, especially those who were pagans or practiced any of the other traditional religions. His Christianization would always remain legendary in its brutality, and few people suffered more than the Basques. The Saxons would also be horrifically oppressed throughout the three decades of war that Charlemagne would wage against them.

The Battle of Roncevaux Pass would become the stuff of legend centuries after the end of Charlemagne's illustrious rule. In the 11th century, 300 years after the battle itself, it became the inspiration for *The Song of Roland*, an epic poem penned by some long-forgotten medieval poet, possibly Turold. The poem, a breathtaking 4,000 lines in length, was hugely popular throughout the late Middle Ages, and it remains the oldest surviving piece of Frankish literature. While its version of events is not fully historical—it glamorizes the Franks as tragic heroes, carefully omitting the brutalities committed against the Basques, and it also includes magical swords and some fictional characters—it remains an impressive and enduring piece of writing.

As for Charlemagne himself, he did not return swiftly to the site of his only defeat, but it remained a thorn in his side for decades. At the turn of the century, however, Charlemagne decided to finally deal with his unfinished business in the Pyrenees. He returned in a series of campaigns and won a belt of territory stretching across the northernmost part of modern-day Spain. This belt would serve as a buffer between Muslim Hispania and Christian Francia, and it became known as the Spanish Marches. It was composed of a series of tiny countries, little more than provinces. Most of these were absorbed by Spain or France at some point in history, now forming modern-day Catalonia, but one of these puny territories still endures as an independent country to this day.

The Principality of Andorra, located right on the border of France and Spain, considers its roots to lie in the edge of Charlemagne's sword. Andorra is a beautiful little place, filled with mountain valleys, and it serves as a hub of tourism and trade, thanks to its low taxes. It has only about half the square mileage of New York City, and its population numbers about the same as the town of Hammond, Indiana (around 77,000 people).

The Children of Hildegard

When Charlemagne returned to win the Spanish Marches around the year 800, he was not alone. In fact, Charlemagne himself did very little of the legwork in that campaign; most of the actual fighting was done by his son, Louis the Pious. Born in 778— the same year that his father suffered the defeat at Roncevaux—Louis was only one of many children that would be born to Charlemagne and his teenage bride, Hildegard.

Hildegard turned out to be a suitably fertile bride, which was highly satisfying to Charlemagne after the disappointment of Desiderata. Hildegard was only fourteen years old when she produced a legitimate heir in 772: a son named Charles the Younger. From there, she would have a child every year for four years running. In 773, she had another son, who was originally named Carloman.

In 774, Charlemagne and Hildegard had their first daughter, Adalheid; she was born during the Siege of Pavia and tragically died on the journey back to Francia. In 775, another daughter would follow, who was named Rotrude. Poor Hildegard would have a short break of a few years then, only giving birth again in 778. As if to make up for it, she had twins this time, both boys. They were named Louis and Lothair, but Lothair tragically died as a baby. The surviving boy, Louis, would become one of Charlemagne's most famous and important sons.

Before Hildegard's death in 784, she would give birth to three more children, all girls, named Bertha, Gisela, and Hildegarde. By the time she died, Hildegard had become the queen of one of the greatest

territories in the whole of Europe. She was a mother to princes, princesses, and even kings. As Charlemagne's kingdom began to grow into an empire, he sought to further consolidate his power by crowning his sons as kings underneath him. In 781, the pope crowned two of Charlemagne's sons. Louis was crowned the king of Aquitaine at the tender age of three years old, while Carloman, aged eight, was crowned the king of Italy. At this point, Carloman was renamed Pepin. This was a clear message from Charlemagne that he considered Pepin to be the rightful heir to his throne. It also perhaps could have been a message saying that he now considered Himiltrude's son, Pepin the Hunchback, to be unworthy of his crown.

Charlemagne's beloved Hildegard turned out to be as perfect a queen as any medieval king could hope for. She accompanied him on most of his campaigns, pregnant and often with small children, enduring the unhappy circumstances of warfare as well as thousands of miles of uncomfortable travel. Having given Charlemagne nine children, she never birthed a stillborn or suffered a miscarriage, at least according to contemporary chroniclers.

Motherhood was not Hildegard's only calling. She was very much involved with the Church and distributed large amounts of her wealth to churches, abbeys, and monasteries. There is also evidence pointing to the fact that Hildegard was more than just a pretty face. Although contemporaries praised her beauty, which they may not have had a choice in doing, considering she was married to the most powerful man in their part of the world, she appears to have been intimately involved in Charlemagne's administration, helping with some of his governmental decisions. Today, some churches consider her a saint.

A horrific blow came to Charlemagne in 783. Hildegard had recently given birth to her last child, a little girl named after her mother. The child was born sometime in 782, and this time, Hildegard's fertility would prove to be her downfall. The queen's youthful body, which had birthed nine babies and was only 25 years old, could take no more. The birth was a traumatic one, and while

Hildegard held on bravely, she ultimately did not survive it. She died on the last day of April and was buried on May Day at an abbey in Metz, where candles were burned on her grave every day for years afterward at Charlemagne's bidding.

Chapter 6 – The Burning of the Sacred Places

Illustration III: Ary Scheffer's 19th*-century depiction of Charlemagne accepting the submission of Widukind at Paderborn.*

September 778 must have been one of the hardest times of Charlemagne's life. A frigid French winter descended upon his army, which was still a long way from home, and they had already traveled the 500 miles from Roncevaux to Auxerre. If Charlemagne was heading to his usual seat at Aachen, he still had 300 miles to go; even if he was going to Paris, he still had 100 miles left to travel. It must have seemed like a very long way to the disheartened Frankish king who'd just buried many of his best commanders and closest friends. He had also just suffered his first and only major defeat.

At Auxerre, Charlemagne began to demobilize his giant army, and we can only imagine that his thoughts were set on the comforts of home. He'd been ruling for ten years and spent most of them in active warfare. But his warring days were far from over. In fact, they were just beginning, and when Charlemagne was at Auxerre, he learned that his fighting for the year was not yet done. Word came to him from the northeast. The Saxons were revolting—again.

The Saxons

This wild, warlike Germanic tribe had been a prolific and intimidating people for centuries. Originating along the North Sea coasts of Germany, the Netherlands, and Denmark, they had threatened all kinds of European powers, from the ancient Romans to the Vikings, and now, they were becoming a thorn in the side of the Carolingian Empire.

Sadly, little is really known about the Saxons and their culture, and their side of history's story has seldom been told. We know that they were named *Saxons* after their choice of weapon: the *seax*, a brutal, short, nimble sword that often spilled the guts of those who considered themselves more civilized, and at close quarters to boot. They spoke a Teutonic language that would become the precursor to the English you're reading right now. Unfortunately for us, the Saxons did not write. They were an illiterate people, and so, their only surviving contemporary histories are those of their enemies.

The earliest records of the Saxons, as with many of these tribes that had no use for the written word, belong to the ancient Romans. As the Roman Empire expanded into Gaul, the Saxons resisted strenuously, and they would be a thorn in the Romans' side until the very end of the empire. Britannica (modern-day Great Britain) was a hotbed for

Roman-Saxon conflict, as the Saxons were expansionists as well. Childeric I, the Merovingian king who fought Attila the Hun alongside the Romans, would be one of many Frankish kings to fight the Saxons. He was a part of one of the last Roman armies to wage war on this fierce tribe.

The Saxons also practiced paganism, worshiping a variety of deities related to the earth and other parts of their surroundings. There are also some parallels with the Norse gods. Trees were particularly important in their religion, as well as Irminsul pillars, sacred monuments to their gods. Sacrifices were important as well, including some instances of human sacrifice. This ancient religion was largely separate from the Christianity that was creeping steadily throughout the world, and it touched every aspect of Saxon culture.

To the growing Roman Catholic Church, the presence of such a large pagan society was practically inexcusable. Widespread efforts were made to convert the Saxons, some of them in the form of peaceful missions, others in oppressive bouts of warfare.

The mission of Boniface was one of the first steps toward the Christianization of Saxony. In the early 8th century, a nobleman from the Christian Saxon Kingdom of Wessex named Wynfrith approached the Roman pope, determined to make a dangerous foray into the heart of the Saxons' country. The pope gave Wynfrith his blessing, changing his name to Boniface.

Boniface was well into his middle age by the time he reached Saxony, but his older age could not suppress his religious zeal. He was described as a blunt man, tactless at times and grumpy, and eager with his ax; he felled numerous sacred Saxon trees. However, Boniface and his followers did not carry weapons.

Building churches wherever he went, Boniface baptized many Saxons, but Christianity didn't quite stick. A group of pagan Saxons fell upon him and his companions deep into Saxony in 754. It is unclear whether they were simply bandits or seeking to destroy this change to their way of life. Either way, the result was the same. The unarmed clergymen were all killed.

As a result, by the time Charlemagne's rule began, the Saxons were still largely pagan. They remained the carbon opposites of the Rome-loving Franks with their literate kings and orderly ways. To make matters worse, the border of Francia and Saxony was poorly defined, often running through open country with no real way for the local people to know which land belonged to the Saxons and which to the Franks. This caused crime and turmoil in the area, as the enemy tribes murdered one another and sabotaged property.

It was clear that the Saxons were a problem that Charlemagne would have to deal with sooner or later. And he did so at the very first opportunity.

The Saxon Wars Begin

In the first few years of his rule, Charlemagne was very much occupied with internal Frankish troubles. The suppression of the Aquitanian rebellion was his first order of business, and it was rapidly followed by his sneaky attempts to get rid of Carloman.

Four years into his reign, though, in 772, things had settled for the young king. Carloman had died, the Aquitanians were thoroughly suppressed, and yet Charlemagne's appetite for warfare and violence was barely getting warmed up. The logical next step was to turn to his most troublesome border, that with Saxony.

Gathering a powerful army, Charlemagne lost no time in marching northeast to Saxony. The Saxons were warlike in their own right, but they stood little chance against Charlemagne's organized army. Few could ever stand against him in a pitched battle; the Saxons, it would appear, had no hope at all. Charlemagne mowed them down, burned their towns, cut down their villages, and finally reached one of their most treasured sites of all: an Irminsul pillar. These great wooden pillars were utterly central to the Saxon faith. Its name meant "world-pillar," and it was related to Yggdrasil, the "world-tree" that anchored and connected all the worlds of the Saxons' belief. To remove that Irminsul pillar was to cut down a great cornerstone of Saxon culture. And that was exactly what Charlemagne did when he came upon one such pillar near Paderborn, the home of the Engrians, whom he beat into submission with the edge of the sword. They were already a defeated people when Charlemagne cut down their pillar. And while many were baptized into Christianity, one must consider that very few of them did this willingly. Perhaps some, having seen their Irminsul fall, clutched at the new hope that was offered them, but many had seen their fellow Saxons die at the edge of Frankish blades and knew that they had no real choice.

Charlemagne's campaign was going well, and he probably could have pushed even farther into Saxony if it was not for the fact that Rome needed him. In 774, he received word from beleaguered Pope Adrian and headed off to fight Desiderius of the Lombards, leaving Saxony to its own devices.

With the great king thus out of the way, the Saxons were finally free to take their revenge, and they did so with desperate violence. Saxon raids were launched on all kinds of Frankish settlements and garrisons. Even the church at Fritzlar, which had been built decades before under the supervision of Boniface himself, was threatened; according to the chroniclers, however, it was miraculously spared from fires. Many other buildings were not so lucky. Franks were killed, their property plundered, and the Saxons felt they were finally taking back what Charlemagne had stolen.

A particularly brutal fight took place when a group of Saxons disguised themselves as Frankish soldiers. They smuggled themselves into the Frankish ranks while their enemies were out on patrol and marched right into the Frankish camp. As soon as the men had let down their guard, the Saxons turned against them and took their revenge. The Franks were taken completely unawares. Many of them were killed before the Saxons made their escape.

Charlemagne, freshly back from subduing the Lombards in 774, was as quick as ever to retaliate against the rebellious Saxons. He rode to the rescue of the Franks, and now that he himself was at the head of his army, it proved to be far more successful against the Saxons. The rebels were beaten back out of the territory that the Franks had claimed. It was clear, though, that the war of 772/73 had not been enough to subdue the rebellious Saxons. Charlemagne would have to formalize his power.

Little did he know that the fight to absorb Saxony into his territory was twenty years away from being over.

A War of Faiths

In 777, a few miles away from the remnants where an Irminsul pillar had once stood, Charlemagne called a great assembly at Paderborn. This was deep within the Saxon territory that the king had claimed, and he demanded the presence of Saxon leaders, ostensibly for diplomatic reasons, but truly, it was clear that Charlemagne was eager to show his power. He wanted the people to know that even their greatest leaders had to be at his beck and call.

And the vast majority of them were. They had already endured five years of violence, and they were ready for peace in their land, even at the cost of freedom. Most of the Saxon rulers were quick to submit to Charlemagne at Paderborn. One, however, was totally absent, a powerful leader named Widukind. Little is really known about this Saxon's life, but he was an adept military commander and a force to be reckoned with in Saxon society, and as such, his rebellion was no small cause for concern. However, he could not be found in the length and breadth of Saxony. He had fled to the Vikings, sheltering with King Sigfred of Denmark, who appears to have been his father-in-law.

At this point in time, Charlemagne was not much bothered with Widukind—an attitude that would prove to be a mistake. But to Charlemagne, what was one rebellious tribal leader now that the entire country was on its knees before him? Content that the assembly of

Paderborn had firmly established him as the supreme ruler over the Saxons, he left once more, this time for the disastrous campaign in Hispania.

So it was that the brokenhearted Charlemagne, grieving the friends and companions that had died at Roncevaux Pass and disassembling his army as winter approached, was disgusted to hear that the Saxons had organized a rebellion once again. And this time, they had fallen upon the Franks with a special depth of hatred that more than matched the brutality with which the Saxons had been treated. This time, their hatred was directed not only to the people who had invaded their country but also to the religion they touted. The Saxons were on a rampage up and down the banks of the Rhine, butchering all in their path, burning churches, and even sexually abusing nuns—an utterly unthinkable act to the Christian mind.

Charlemagne was immediately incensed. Despite the fact that winter was approaching and his army was exhausted from its hard defeat and long march home, he could not allow the Saxons to keep wreaking havoc on his people and their culture. The main body of the army had already scattered back home, but Charlemagne's own bodyguard was still with him. This powerful regiment likely consisted of strong cavalry that could travel swiftly and also pack an enormous punch, the precursors of the knights that would emerge later in the Middle Ages. They were known as the *scara*, and they stood ever ready to do the king's bidding.

Although Charlemagne himself would remain in Francia, the *scara* rode as fast as their horses would take them to the border of Saxony. After arriving in the "barbarian" land, the *scara* fell upon the Saxons with swift brutality. Despite their relatively small numbers, the Franks succeeded in putting an end to the Saxon rampage. It would be Charlemagne's only real victory for the year of 778.

It must have been a good one, though, because 779 brought about the beginning of the end for the Saxons. The *scara* alone had wrought so much havoc on the Saxons in battle that they were beginning to realize that fighting Charlemagne would be a foolish endeavor. When Charlemagne returned to Saxony that year, tribes from all over the country came to see him, seeking to give him their submission and asking to be baptized and allowed to live in peace. Again, some of them may truly have decided to convert to Christianity, but it's not difficult to assume that most of them were simply motivated by fear. If they submitted to Charlemagne and gave up their religion, at least they would be allowed to live in something resembling peace. Some of these tribes had never even met with Charlemagne before; they had only heard of what he'd done to their fellow countrymen and decided to choose surrender over war.

After that, Charlemagne appears again to have decided that the trouble in Saxony was finally at an end. In 780 and 781, he was occupied with Frankish affairs and traveled to Rome in order to have Pepin and Louis the Pious crowned as the kings of Italy and Aquitaine. (Charles the Younger would be made king of the Franks in 800.) He would only turn his attention back to Saxony in 782. This time, it would be done more peacefully. After all, the Saxons had been largely peaceful for several years by this point, not daring to show any resistance to the Franks after the violence they'd experienced at the hands of the *scara* in 778.

Charlemagne decided that it was time to hold another assembly and check on his relations with the Saxon leaders. Perhaps this time, even Widukind would be brought to heel. These hopes, however, were unfounded. Many Saxon leaders came in submission, but Widukind was a no-show, and riding through the Saxon countryside, Charlemagne could see that the people at large were not quite as subdued as their leaders. Little knots of Saxon rebels were everywhere, no doubt hoping for Widukind to return from Denmark with an impressive Viking army and overthrow this arrogant Frank once and for all. In fact, there were rumors in Saxony that Widukind had already returned and was summoning an army to stand against Charlemagne.

Still, there was little cause yet for Charlemagne to actually fight battles against them. That was until the year 782, a year in which Charlemagne would show his darkest side.

Beyond Saxony, there were more Germanic tribes that continued to live in freedom, and these were constantly rebelling along Charlemagne's new Saxon border. These rebellions, however, were small and easily crushed by Charlemagne's noblemen without his personal involvement. One such nobleman was Count Theodoric, the head of a small portion of Charlemagne's army that included numerous noblemen who were not only high-ranking officials but also close companions to Charlemagne himself. Still, they were men of war, and both they and Charlemagne thought nothing of it when he asked them to ride out against one such rebelling tribe and suppress them.

En route to the border, Count Theodoric came across a different enemy than he'd bargained for. Widukind really was back in Saxony again, and he was causing trouble wherever he went. Most recently, he'd stirred up a group of Saxons who had formerly submitted to Charlemagne. They found Theodoric as he rode merrily off to war. Accounts differ on what exactly happened next. Some write that the Saxons fell upon Theodoric in a surprise attack reminiscent of the ambush at Roncevaux Pass. Others say that Theodoric came across the rebels, perhaps during a minor skirmish, and began to make plans to go out against them. Before he could do so, however, some of the minor lords in his employ decided that they'd do it themselves. They were loath to lose all of the glory of battle to Theodoric himself and decided that they'd win themselves some honor. Instead, they found nothing but death and defeat at the hands of the Saxons.

Charging out against the Saxons in disarray and without their most capable commander, Theodoric's men found themselves briskly surrounded, outnumbered, and then killed by the thousands. It was a bloody battlefield that day; even Count Theodoric himself, perhaps as part of the onslaught or perhaps in an attempt to rescue his endangered men, was killed. It was a horrible defeat for the Franks at the hands of Widukind, and once again, it was a crushing blow for Charlemagne.

Only four years after the stinging tragedy that had been Roncevaux, Charlemagne was once more confronted with grief, loss, and humiliation by the deaths of so many of his noblemen and friends. He was enraged at the fact that this barbarian rabble had been able to take so much from him. This was, after all, the Middle Ages; inequality was part and parcel of life there, and the idea that some lives were infinitely more valuable than others governed every aspect of society. To Charlemagne, the death of Count Theodoric was worse than the loss of a thousand ordinary soldiers. And it was abundantly clear that the Franks already viewed the Saxons as inferior.

Before Charlemagne could summon his men and ride out against the Saxons, their own people stepped forward to solve the problem. Petrified that Charlemagne's wrath against Widukind would have devastating repercussions for their own peaceful people, many of the Saxons that had allied themselves with Charlemagne took it upon themselves to identify and capture the rebels. They brought thousands of rebels to Verden, where they would await Charlemagne's judgment.

The king's next action is one that is almost inconceivable in the sheer scope of its violence and wanton destruction of human life. Perhaps one can attempt to delve into the psychology of this decision. Emotion was not something that medieval kings were taught how to deal with; grief was an everyday part of their experience, and as men, they were expected to keep a stiff upper lip and never allow this pain to show. But Roncevaux had struck Charlemagne deeply, much more deeply than simply causing him humiliation. He had never been allowed to process the deep personal losses he had suffered that day. Instead, they had festered like an abscess on his soul, and that abscess had burst with the death of Theodoric. Overwhelmed by helpless rage and unspeakable bereavement, Charlemagne turned to violence.

Perhaps this move could be thought of as political. The Saxons had been a thorn in Charlemagne's side for ten years. Making an example out of these rebels might put an end to years of war and ultimately allow him to seek greater territories to conquer.

Still, it's impossible to justify what Charlemagne did next, much less understand it. The king reacted in a movement of unspeakable violence that can hardly be comprehended, one that rivals many of the bloodiest moments in history and which speaks powerfully to the dangers of absolute power. Faced with thousands of Saxon rebels, unarmed and bound, Charlemagne decided that there was only one way to deal with them. They would all be killed—and not only killed but gorily beheaded. All of them, in a single day.

Four thousand five hundred men died that day, creating a scene of carnage that is almost impossible to imagine, let alone describe. The swish and chop of axes or swords slicing human heads from their shoulders must have filled the air. The amount of blood must have been nearly unthinkable, spurting, running, pooling, soaking into the earth, a stain on the memory of that place forever. Thousands of Frankish soldiers were employed to carry out the dark deed. One is almost afraid to imagine the screams, the pleas for mercy, the horror in the hearts of those waiting to die as they watched their compatriots being butchered like sheep in a gruesome manner that was robbed of any semblance of dignity.

The scope of Charlemagne's awful massacre is so vast and the logistics so complicated (how do you kill 4,500 people, one by one, in a single day?), that many historians dispute whether it ever actually happened. Thanks to Saxon illiteracy, the only contemporary account is found in the royal Frankish annals, which may have employed a degree of hyperbole in order to make Charlemagne seem more terrible and glorious. However, there is little reason to doubt that Charlemagne's treatment of the Saxons was intensely brutal. By 782, they were a broken and defeated people.

Widukind himself, however, was not part of the army killed at Verden. He had escaped once more, fleeing again to his Viking allies.

Decades of Warfare

If it had been Charlemagne's hope to end the Saxon Wars with the Massacre of Verden, then he had spilled the blood of 4,500 people in vain. The Saxon Wars were a long way from over, thanks in part to the survival of Widukind.

Having committed this unspeakable atrocity—one bordering on genocide—against the Saxon people, Charlemagne's next step was to consolidate his power in a more orderly manner. He had struck terror into the hearts of the Saxons; now, he had to show them what it meant to live under a Frankish king. He sat down to compose a set of laws that would dictate the Saxons' new way of life, including restrictions on the religion they were allowed to practice. In short, any form of paganism was punishable by death, although a suitably repentant transgressor could be pardoned by a priest. The Saxons had no choice at all. Or rather, they had an impossible one: they could uphold Christian traditions or die.

In secular areas, however, the Saxons were allowed to keep their traditional laws. The Franks characteristically did not interfere much with the everyday secular trespasses of their subjected peoples, allowing them to maintain their old laws as long as they converted to Christianity.

Still, in that time, law and religion were almost inextricably linked. Robbing the Saxons of their own belief system was a fundamental change to their entire culture and way of life, one that most of them had not willingly chosen. Bursts of sporadic rebellions continued across Saxony.

However, during 783, Charlemagne was much too occupied to launch another campaign against them. This turned out to be a year of yet more loss and personal tragedy for him. It was the year in which he lost the woman who had been a pillar of his present life and guarantee of his dynasty's future: Hildegard. To make matters worse, that same year, his mother also died. Bertrada had been more than Charlemagne's mother; she had been an important, albeit unofficial, adviser to him. The two most important women in his life were lost to him within a year. And since he'd lost so many of his closest allies at Roncevaux and in Saxony, Charlemagne found himself feeling lost.

He moved fast, however, to remarry, even though Hildegard had given him numerous viable heirs. Charlemagne's quick remarriage was unlikely to have been a move to secure the future of his family's rule. Instead, he was struggling to cement his power in the present. The woman he married is little known to history, but we do know that her name was Fastrada and that she came from East Francia. This wedding was undoubtedly a political move. Although the chroniclers attest that he and Fastrada had an emotional bond, an alliance with a powerful East Francian family would strengthen Charlemagne's war with Saxony. Fastrada would give him two daughters during their marriage, Theodrada and Hiltrude, both of whom became abbesses.

Charlemagne couldn't waste much time in picking himself up from the latest losses in his life, for he had to return to Saxony in order to put an end to the continuous rebellions there. He rode out against the Saxons in 784, and for the first time, he was accompanied by one of his sons in this campaign. Charles the Younger was only twelve years old, but medieval society already considered him a man. Maturity had to come quickly for medieval princes, and it was time for him to prove himself as a worthy successor to the warrior king who had fathered him.

The campaign Charles joined turned out to be a long and difficult one. Widukind was back in Saxony, fighting tooth and nail alongside his renewed band of rebels. The Franks truly had their work cut out for them in suppressing the many small flames of revolt that flickered all across the country. Widukind was likely outnumbered and under-resourced, but he was an excellent strategist, and he kept the Carolingian commanders on their toes. Widukind's rebellion was so powerful that Charlemagne would not see his home all year. Instead, he took a risky decision and remained in Saxony throughout the winter, sending his men out to fight in the bitter cold and blowing snow. It was a baptism through fire for young Charles. His armor already hung heavy on his youthful shoulders, and now, he had to deal with it in the freezing cold as well.

Charlemagne's hard decision paid off. Slowly, the Franks ground away at the Saxon resistance until even its leader could no longer keep fighting. In 785, Widukind finally gave up. He surrendered and pleaded with Charlemagne for a promise that he wouldn't be harmed if he turned himself in. Charlemagne gave his solemn word, and Widukind courageously, considering what Charlemagne had done with his last set of prisoners, went before him.

Perhaps the screams of Verden were still ringing in Charlemagne's ears, and maybe there was some kind of regret in his heart for what he had done. Instead of harming Widukind, Charlemagne kept his promise. The rebel leader was baptized into Christianity, and from there, he disappears from history. It's possible to speculate that he, too, may have ended up cloistered in some forgotten monastery, living out his life in peace but not freedom.

Such would eventually be the fate of Saxony itself. Even though Widukind was conquered in 785, it would be almost twenty years before the Saxon Wars would be declared over, although the scale of violence was much diminished compared to the first decade of warfare. Some hope came to the Saxons in 793 when Denmark decided to get involved and the Vikings began to raid the Franks; however, these forces were defeated so soundly that Saxon refugees were no longer able to enter Denmark in 798. It was the beginning of the end for the Saxons, and the last rebellion took place in 804. After that, Saxony officially belonged to Charlemagne. It had become yet another piece of his kingdom, a kingdom that had now grown into something even bigger. Something that would, by the time the Saxon Wars were over, grow into an empire.

Chapter 7 – More Conquests

Illustration IV: A golden bust of Charlemagne.

The conquest of Saxony was still not enough for the growing appetite of this expansionist ruler. In fact, even while he was still waging the Saxon Wars, Charlemagne was already seeking other territories to conquer.

As his sons grew into what counted for manhood in the Middle Ages, Charlemagne was supported by them as he sought to expand his lands. Louis, king of Aquitaine, was sent to campaign in the south, where he eventually won most of Spain. Pepin was campaigning on the borders of Italy, while Charles the Younger fought with his father in Saxony. Charlemagne's empire began to expand in all directions, wreaking devastation on the surrounding peoples. But first, there was some conquering to be done within Francia itself.

The Bloodless Bavarian Conquest

Duke Tassilo III of Bavaria had been Charlemagne's rival ever since he was a little boy.

His father, Duke Odilo of Bavaria, had long been a friend of Charles's father, Pepin the Short. More than that, Odilo was family. He had married Pepin's sister (Charles Martel's daughter), forming a powerful alliance between the dukes of Bavaria and the mayors of the Frankish palace. When Pepin became a king, the alliance still held firm.

Yet power and alliances in the Middle Ages were always tenuous at best, as they were always just one dead nobleman away from crumbling, and things fell apart in 748, the same year that Charlemagne was born. Tassilo, Odilo's son, was only seven years old at the time. He was left orphaned and alone, and Pepin was quick to take the boy into his own household and raise him as a ward of the Frankish royalty. While family compassion may have played some role in Pepin's decision, he undoubtedly also saw an opportunity. By raising Bavaria's rightful duke, Pepin had a trump card up his sleeve if Bavaria itself should ever slip through his fingers.

This was exactly what happened nine years later when Grifo, Pepin's illegitimate brother, attempted to seize Bavaria. Sixteen-year-old Tassilo was abruptly thrust into his role as the duke of Bavaria, and Pepin ousted Grifo, placing Tassilo on the throne instead. The boy had been raised as if he was a son of Pepin's, so it was no difficult task to make him a vassal to Pepin, thus effectively securing Bavaria as Pepin's territory.

Tassilo appears to have been quite content with this arrangement, which was fairly usual for the time. He married one of Desiderius's daughters, forming a strong alliance with the Lombards, and also had a fairly good relationship with the pope.

Things grew sour for Tassilo in 763 when he was a grown man and Pepin was at war with Aquitaine. The Frankish king called on Tassilo to help him, but the latter had alliances with some Aquitanian nobles who were in revolt. He was unwilling to go to war against them and declined to come to Pepin's aid, even though, as he was Pepin's vassal, he had already sworn fealty to the king many years ago. Abandoning Pepin to his fate, Tassilo may have indirectly helped cause the king's death five years later.

This obviously complicated Tassilo's relationship with Charlemagne. The two rulers had grown up in the palace together, and just as Carloman must have always felt a few steps behind his older brother, Charlemagne would have grown up resenting Tassilo. The young man was always much further ahead in his education as a ruler and a warrior than Charlemagne was simply because he was seven years older. One can imagine that this chafed Charlemagne's budding ego. He was, after all, the crown prince of Francia; why should he be made to feel so inferior to some simple duke?

Thus, there was likely some rivalry brewing between Charlemagne and Tassilo, one that Charlemagne would not forget even after he had proven himself to be the greatest king that Francia had ever seen. Added to this, Charlemagne had lost Pepin the Short when he was still a young man, and the memory of his father's tragic early death still stung. In grief, he may have been looking for someone to blame, and Tassilo was a handy scapegoat. Perhaps if the Bavarian duke had ridden to Pepin's aid—the man who had raised Tassilo and given him power and a title—when the former king had asked, then Charlemagne's father would have lived to fight another day.

Either way, Charlemagne clearly wanted Tassilo out, and he wanted Bavaria for himself as well. To take over the duchy legally, he would have to get help—and that help would have to come from Pope Adrian. Only Adrian could declare Tassilo as unfit to rule, thus allowing Charlemagne to take over Bavaria without force and without damaging the territory he wanted to claim for himself.

Luckily for Charlemagne, the pope was no friend of Tassilo. His relationship with Tassilo had been fairly good, but Tassilo had not been as quick as Charlemagne to repudiate his Lombard wife. Accordingly, when Adrian needed help against the marauding Lombards, Tassilo had not responded.

In 788, with things quietening down on the Saxon front, Charlemagne decided that it was time to deal with his old rival. He approached the pope for help, and Adrian quickly declared Tassilo an oath-breaker thanks to his failure to support Pepin in the Aquitanian campaign. Tassilo was thus unfit to rule. His titles were stripped from him, and he was packed off to a monastery, Charlemagne's favorite solution for troublesome nobility. All of Tassilo's rights to Bavaria were formally handed over to Charlemagne in 794, and the duchy was divided up into small counties and became a part of Francia.

The Fall of the Great Ring

As Saxony was assimilated into Charlemagne's growing empire, the Franks found themselves coming into contact with more and more "barbarian" tribes as their borders pushed out farther. One such tribe, and perhaps one of the most formidable, was the Avars.

This nomadic Asian tribe, which consisted of quite diverse peoples, had been ruling over the steppes of Asia and Eastern Europe for centuries. After the fall of Attila and the end of the Hunnic Empire, the Avars had been quick to flow into the power vacuum that Attila left behind, and they rapidly proved themselves worthy of being his successor. Like the Huns, they were adept horsemen who consistently used stirrups long before their neighbors, a considerable advantage as having stirrups on the saddles of their swift warhorses allowed them greater stability and speed. Thus, they could fire arrows from the backs of galloping horses with immense accuracy. They were also one of the first people to use the trebuchet, which would become an important part of siege warfare in medieval Europe.

By 626, the Avars were powerful enough that they laid siege to Constantinople. They built a truly impressive fortress known as the Great Ring of the Avars, possibly located in modern-day Austria, east of Bavaria. The Ring was made of several concentric circles of wooden fortifications, with archers and other warriors in between the circles. It was a formidable fortress indeed, and the Avars ruled powerfully from within it, building a great empire.

The Avar Empire, like many others of its kind, was short-lived. Internal squabbles chipped away at its power, and by the late 8th century, it was crumbling badly. Nonetheless, the Avars did not give up on expanding their collapsing lands. They turned on Bavaria and Friuli in 788 and launched a destructive invasion.

Charlemagne had just claimed Bavaria that same year, but trouble in Saxony called him away, forcing him to allow his new lands to languish in the hands of the Avars for two long years. It was only in 790 that he could finally strike back against these fierce nomads. Along with his son, Pepin Carloman, and a powerful commander known as Duke Eric of Friuli, Charlemagne attacked the Avars.

Pepin and Eric worked together to attack the Great Ring itself, and despite its impressive fortifications, it fell before the might of the Frankish army. Cutting through all the way into the heart of the Ring,

Pepin and Eric discovered a rich reward for their efforts. The Avars had been collecting booty for centuries, including some from the Frankish territories they'd so recently lost, and the central ring of the Great Ring was absolutely stuffed with gold. Charlemagne had returned to his favored seat at Aachen by this time, but Pepin proudly sent him a staggering amount of gold and treasure stolen from the Avars.

The Great Ring would not remain long in Frankish possession. It eventually fell back into the hands of the Avars, but the days of the Avar Empire were numbered. By 795, the tuduns, or governors, had realized that they were fighting a losing battle that would only cost their people in money and blood. They journeyed to meet with Charlemagne and turned themselves over as his vassals, offering him their surrender and allowing themselves to be baptized into the Roman Catholic Church.

In the process of baptizing the tuduns, Charlemagne selected one of them to become a new ruler, bestowing upon him the title of khagan, an ancient name for an Avar ruler. Khagan Abraham, who had received his new name from Charlemagne, was sent back to rule the Avars as vassals of the Frankish king. Thus, the Avar Empire officially ended in 796.

Trust between the Avars and the Franks, however, remained very tenuous. Charlemagne soon lost confidence in Khagan Abraham and led a personal assault on the Great Ring of the Avars. The fortress fell before him for the last time, signaling the end of the Avars as a whole.

There was a small rebellion sometime later, around 799, as some Avars mustered against the Franks and sallied out for their freedom. It must have felt like a noble idea to the Avars, who longed for their old way of life, but it was an ill-conceived one. Charlemagne sent a Bavarian army out against them. The Avars were defeated, the confederation of Avar tribes came to an end, and even the Avar race itself eventually intermingled with the Franks and died out.

The Defeat of the Slavs

Charlemagne's treatment of the tribes surrounding his empire was deplorable, as it often led to the end of entire races. The Slavs, however, was one tribe that he never managed to stamp out. Even though the Slavs were illiterate and their origins wreathed in mystery, their language is the root of many influential languages still widely spoken today, including Russian and Polish.

But in the 8th century, the Slavs were no one in particular, especially not to the "civilized" world. Even the ancient Romans had barely documented them, dismissing them as just another tribe of barbarians that had to be subjugated. For this reason, we know very little about the early Slavs. They may have been nomadic, and they may have originated in modern-day Poland or the Czech Republic. Either way, they were definitely pagans in the eyes of Charlemagne. They were polytheists who worshiped many gods that had similarities to the faith of the Vikings, including a ruling god of thunder and important gods of love and fertility. Although, where the Norse gods typically were more or less human in shape, the Slavic gods had many heads—as many as four in the case of their god of war.

By the time of Charlemagne's empire, the Slavs had replaced the Huns in the Balkans. They had some alliances with—and similarities to—the Avars, but they operated as an independent people, often fractured in their approach to the Franks. Still, they controlled vast tracts of territory, and there was nothing that Charlemagne hungered after more than new lands.

By 789, even though he was still busy conquering the Saxons, Charlemagne had already drafted vast numbers of them into his army. The warlike race that he had to spend thirty years conquering proved to be as valuable in his army as they had been destructive fighting against it. Eager to test out his new soldiers on some unsuspecting tribe, Charlemagne decided that the Slavs were a logical next step.

Marching the Saxons into Slavic territory, Charlemagne crossed the Rhine and moved into foreign lands that he was determined to own.

The Slavs were met with the glittering ranks of Charlemagne's breathtaking army, and they wisely offered little to no resistance, capitulating quickly in the face of Charlemagne's power. He traveled across Slavic territory all the way to the shores of the Baltic. And everywhere he trod, he decided that he owned the land.

Interestingly, although the Slavs were pagans, Charlemagne was far gentler with them than he had been with the Saxons. His violent Christianization of Saxony was not repeated here in the Slavic territories. Perhaps the bloodshed at Verden had left him with regrets, or perhaps he had simply seen that that level of violence had caused more trouble in Saxony in the end than it was worth. Either way, there is little to attest to any particularly brutal treatment of the Slavs from Charlemagne's side. Instead, when they submitted to him, he simply demanded the right to send missionaries into their lands and ordered that those missionaries, who were usually peaceful and unarmed people, should be left unharmed.

There was more to conquering the Slavs than simply gaining more land and power, however. The Slavs themselves would prove to be strong allies who stood by Charlemagne with fidelity and courage as he continued his expansion.

Of course, not all of the Slavs surrendered to Charlemagne without a fight. He divided the new territory into duchies as he had done with most of his lands, and one of these, Littoral, was filled with rebels who refused to bend the knee to this foreign king. Their rebellion turned out to be a failure, however, as their own people turned against them and fought on Charlemagne's side. Pannonian and Dalmatian Slavs joined forces with Charlemagne to fight those from Littoral, located in modern-day Croatia.

Still, the Littoral Slavs were able to cause plenty of grief and trouble for the Franks, even though their rebellion was ultimately doomed. During the long and gruesome Siege of Trsat in 799, Eric of Friuli, the duke who had proven to be one of Charlemagne's most adept commanders, was killed. It was a terrible loss for Charlemagne, both personally and in terms of his empire; the experienced Eric had been an invaluable strategist, as well as a useful adviser to the young Pepin Carloman.

The Span of the Carolingian Empire

By the early 800s, Charlemagne was ruling over a truly vast territory that stretched all the way from Spain to Scandinavia, from the British Channel to the Baltic Sea. He had conquered a huge variety of peoples, from the Slavs to the Saxons, the Avars to the Aquitanians, and the Basques to the Umayyads.

His rule extended over thirteen modern-day countries: Austria, Croatia, Belgium, Slovenia, Liechtenstein, France, Spain, Switzerland, Andorra, the Netherlands, Italy, Luxembourg, and the Czech Republic. The unity of this vast realm had been unheard-of since the days of the Western Roman Empire. In fact, it's considered that Charlemagne's empire was the hammer and forge that forced the glowing metal of a scattered and uneducated part of the world into the cold, sharp steel that Europe would become in the centuries to follow.

The forging of this mighty dominion would later earn Charlemagne another title: Father of Europe. What was more, he was the first to tout the idea of Christendom, of a vast array of Christian lands united in their religion. It can be argued that his vision never truly came to pass. However, Charlemagne was filled with high ideals, and these would endure into the Middle Ages that followed. The dynamics of power and spirituality that Charlemagne introduced through his strong bonds with the pope, even as he unified vast tracts of land, would give birth to much of medieval culture—including, arguably, the Crusades.

Charlemagne was no longer just a king. The "King of the Franks and Lombards" had grown into something bigger, as the lands he controlled became something far more than a mere kingdom. With kings bowing down at his feet to do him homage, Charlemagne had grown into something that Western Europe hadn't seen since the fall of the Western Roman Empire in the 5th century.

Charlemagne had become an emperor. And it would only be a matter of time before that title was officially bestowed upon him by the only man who had that kind of power: the Roman Catholic pope himself.

Chapter 8 – An Empire Rises

Illustration V: Jean-Victor Schnetz's painting of Charlemagne and Alcuin of York, completed in 1830. It hangs in the Louvre today.

As the 8th century drew to a close, Charlemagne had become one of the most powerful people in Europe. He had unified a truly vast territory and ruled over a vast population of many diverse peoples. Even though he had shown great brutality in his conquests, he had also proven himself to be a capable administrator, as well as an adept warrior.

In fact, Charlemagne's territory was no longer a mere kingdom. It stretched over many kingdoms, and it could easily be called an empire. But for that to happen, Charlemagne would have to become an emperor.

The Roman Need for an Emperor

Charlemagne's assistance of Pope Adrian I against the Lombards in 774 had been the start of more than two decades of peace and prosperity in Rome. With the greatest king in Europe as the bodyguard of his reign, Adrian had very little to fear. No one would dare to invade his lands, not with Charlemagne backing him. Added to that, the constant stream of revenue into Charlemagne's hands was often diverted into the coffers of the Roman Catholic Church. It was a very good time to be the pope.

It would be a mistake, however, to view Adrian as Charlemagne's lap dog. Even though the pope needed Charlemagne's protection militarily, he still maintained a fiercely independent mindset, and he proved himself to be an outstanding politician. Employing peaceful diplomacy and making careful alliances, Adrian was able to greatly expand the Papal States. And where Charlemagne protected Rome, Adrian played no small role in protecting Charlemagne's budding empire. He worked hard to maintain peaceful relations with the Byzantine Empire by supporting its position on iconoclasm when he personally attended the Council of Nicaea in 787.

Adrian's relationship with Charlemagne was often tinged with rivalry. He was not always happy about Charlemagne's extensive influence over Italian lands, and tensions could arise between them when it came to Roman matters. Despite this, however, his personal relationship with Charlemagne was a close one. He might not have had Charlemagne's military strength, but he had more wisdom and experience than the king, and for twenty years, Charlemagne cherished their friendship.

That golden age for Rome came to an end in 795. Adrian, whose birthdate is unknown but who would have been quite elderly by this time, passed away due to natural causes in the winter of that year. When the news reached Charlemagne, who was leading a campaign against the Avars at the time, he was deeply saddened. In fact, he composed—by dictation—a long and poetic epitaph to Adrian, which can be seen today in the Vatican. The epitaph is a testimony to Charlemagne's close relationship with the pope; in it, he even refers to him as "father." It might not be too much to say that Adrian really did act as a father figure in Charlemagne's life, considering that the two men became friends six years after Charlemagne's loss of Pepin the Short.

Not all of the Romans, however, shared quite the same love for Charlemagne that Adrian had. Fearing that the king would attempt to interfere with the papal succession as Desiderius had done, the Romans were quick to elect a new pope. In fact, on the very day that Adrian died, the cardinal-priest of St. Susanna was consecrated as Pope Leo III.

Leo was not quite as independently-minded as Adrian had been. Aware of Adrian and Charlemagne's relationship, and eager not to make an enemy out of the powerful warrior king, he sent an envoy to Aachen with the standard of the city and the keys of the confession of St. Peter. In a roundabout symbolic way, Leo was sending Charlemagne a message that said he saw the king as the protector of Rome. Charlemagne, while deeply grieving Adrian, was ready to make friends with Leo. He sent Leo a letter that congratulated him on his recent ascension to pope, along with a large amount of treasure that had just recently been seized from the Great Ring of the Avars.

With Charlemagne backing him, Leo felt he had little to fear, and for four years, this proved to be true. But trouble brewed in Rome nonetheless. Leo's election had ostensibly been unanimous, but he was not the only papal candidate. A member of Adrian's family had also been considered, and he had many supporters. These grew more and more restless with Leo in charge of Rome. And with Charlemagne occupied with squashing an Avar rebellion in 799, they decided that there was little the Frankish ruler could do to stop them.

In the spring of 799, Leo was part of a ritual procession as he celebrated the Greater Litanies. He headed for Rome's Flaminian Gate in all his pomp and splendor as cheering crowds of Romans surrounded him. He'd been the pope for several years and was settling happily into his role, invincible under Charlemagne's protection. Or so he thought.

Without warning, a group of armed men burst from the crowd, rushing down upon the weaponless pope. Leo didn't stand a chance. He was seized and thrown to the ground, and they fell upon him with brutal violence, their hands scratching and clawing at his face. Their aim was not to kill him; it was simply to mutilate him, to make him unfit to be pope. They scrabbled at his eyes and mouth, hoping to put out his eyes and rip out his tongue. Leo's supporters were woefully inadequate. They did little to save him, and while his attackers were ultimately unsuccessful in their attempts, Leo was left alone and bleeding in the street for some time.

When nightfall came, the unconscious, wounded pope was still lying in the street. His supporters came to pick him up then and carried him off to a nearby monastery, where he recovered.

After having regained his strength, Leo realized that his protectors within Rome itself could do nothing to keep him safe from his opposition. It was an automatic reflex to turn to the man who'd been Rome's guardian angel for decades: Charlemagne. Along with a group of Roman sympathizers, Leo hurried over the Alps that summer, joining Charlemagne at Paderborn.

Of course, Charlemagne was quick to help Leo, although he could not personally journey to Rome at that time. He sent an envoy with Leo to put him back into his rightful place in the Vatican, and they returned him to Rome unmolested, then went on to search for those who had attacked him in order to imprison them. They were thrown into a dungeon to await a trial the following year when Charlemagne himself could attend to the matter.

A Christmas Coronation

When the next year came, Charlemagne had arranged his affairs so that he could journey to Rome again, visiting it perhaps for the first time since the death of Adrian. He presided over the trial of the accused who had attacked Leo. In turn, they brought charges of adultery and perjury against Leo. They could provide no evidence of Leo's guilt, but the pope was still desperate to prove himself worthy in the eyes of the people, and so, he swore a lengthy oath of innocence to Charlemagne. This was a humiliating thing to do, but it worked. The accused were condemned to death, and Leo won Roman hearts when he petitioned for them to be exiled instead of killed. Charlemagne agreed, and Leo was able to take his place as pope once more without opposition.

Still, Leo had been shaken by these events, both emotionally and politically. His enemies had been dealt with, but he wasn't sure that the Romans had much faith in him. He lacked the personal friendship that Adrian had enjoyed with Charlemagne, and he needed to do something to cement Frankish-Roman relations. So, he hatched a plan, one that likely did not have much of Charlemagne's involvement, but one that would change his life and the course of history forever.

Charlemagne had decided to remain in Rome for the winter, celebrating Christmas in the splendor of St. Peter's. Christmas Mass at Rome in the Middle Ages was always a wonderful spectacle, filled with ceremony and celebration. St. Peter's was packed with people, many of them Europe's most important dignitaries, but none were more important than Charlemagne.

Charlemagne's biographer, Einhard, who wrote extensively on the subject of the ruler's life from 817 to 830, claimed that despite Charlemagne's tremendous power, he seldom indulged in dressing up. Usually, he wore a linen shirt, silk tunic, and otter-skin cloak as any ordinary Frankish nobleman would wear; only rarely did he don the more elaborate ceremonial garb. Still, he was a majestic sight when he did. His towering height of six feet, three inches would be tall today; in the 9th century, when the average adult male stood only five feet, eight inches, it was tremendous. On Christmas Day, Charlemagne was decked out in a flowing blue cloak that poured over his still-powerful frame, fastened by a giant golden buckle. Rich embroidery covered his clothes, jewels glittered on his fingers and at his throat, and the hilt of his sword was made of expensive metal, shimmering with precious stones.

He was a breathtaking sight as he strode up to the altar. Decades of war had given him a slight limp, and the hair that curled richly around his head was turning white, but he still exuded power and charisma. Kneeling down in prayer at the richly decorated altar, the king bowed his head.

There is a debate among historians today if he was aware of what was about to happen. Einhard says that Leo's next action was a complete surprise to Charlemagne, although others argue that he must have at least suspected that Leo had some scheme in the works. Either way, it was a splendid, unorthodox, and history-making moment. Leo strode up behind the kneeling and bareheaded king. Seizing a brilliantly decorated crown, the pope cried out, "To Charles, the most pious Augustus, crowned by God, the great and peace-giving Emperor, life and victory!" He repeated these words twice, and they rang throughout St. Peter's as he lowered the great crown on Charlemagne's white head.

Before Charlemagne could rise, Leo fell to his knees and began to anoint Charlemagne's feet with oil. Cheers broke out, and the clergymen who were present began to recite the coronation litany. With that, Charlemagne had become the emperor of Rome.

In practice, becoming emperor didn't add any lands to Charlemagne's dominion. He was effectively ruling over most of the old Western Roman Empire already thanks to his many conquests.

Still, it had been more than 300 years since the last time an emperor ruled over Italy, and this new title ushered Charlemagne's lands into a new era: the era of a great empire. He was no longer simply the king of the Franks and Lombards but an emperor of a territory now known as the Carolingian Empire.

Leo's act of crowning Charlemagne had many motivations, which are still the subject of debate amongst historians, and also many repercussions, which would resound throughout thousands of years of history. One of the most immediate consequences was the conflict with the Byzantines. The Eastern Roman Empire was being ruled by Empress Irene, whose claim to the throne was shaky already and invalid—at least in the eyes of Charlemagne and Leo—because she was a woman. Under the traditional Salic law that was a simple fact of life for these men, women were simply unfit to rule. In Leo's eyes, he had crowned Charlemagne not as emperor over the western half of the Roman Empire but over the Roman Empire as a whole. Empress Irene was not amused, and considering she held territory as close to Charlemagne's borders as Venice, this was a considerable threat—one that would cost Charlemagne dearly in the years to come.

But for the first decade of Charlemagne's rule as Roman emperor, he turned much of his warfare over to his sons, and he was able to settle down and concentrate on administration. And here, he would prove to be so much more than just a military genius. Age had tempered the great man's rage somewhat, and he turned to making his empire a hotbed of culture, arts, and learning, resulting in a powerful resurgence of these gentler areas of life that would be known as the Carolingian Renaissance.

The Carolingian Renaissance

Now that he bore the same title as the rulers of ancient Rome, Charlemagne seemed to feel that he owed them a debt, and he felt obliged to revive and preserve their ideas, writings, and culture. The Carolingian Empire quickly began to grow into something reminiscent of ancient Rome, and this dive into culture and learning would not be seen again until after the Middle Ages.

One of Charlemagne's first steps was to standardize the currency used in his realm, basing this new currency on that of ancient Rome. His *livre carolinienne, sous,* and *deniers* were modeled on ancient Rome's *libra, solidus,* and *denarius,* and they would eventually become the modern-day pound, shilling, and penny. These coins were used throughout his empire, facilitating much easier trade. Measurements were also standardized, making communication easier. Perhaps for the first time, the subjugated peoples of the Germanic tribes he'd conquered were able to enjoy some benefits of being part of Charlemagne's domain.

Charlemagne also seemed to be trying to turn Aachen into a second Rome, as the architecture of the buildings he commissioned there—and elsewhere in his empire—was strongly reminiscent of Roman antiquity. The breathtaking Palatine Chapel, built in 792 and Charlemagne's personal place of worship in Aachen, is only one example.

However, it was not in architecture or currency that Charlemagne's greatest influence lay. Although he was also a patron of the arts and music, his deepest passion was for education and literature.

Alcuin of York, a British scholar, was one of Charlemagne's most beloved and trusted advisers and also one of the most influential educators of his time. Charlemagne gave Alcuin everything he needed to turn Aachen into a blossoming center of learning. In a time when even the most highborn people seldom learned to read or write, Charlemagne made waves by having Alcuin compose a standardized curriculum, bringing literacy and education all over the length and breadth of the Carolingian Empire.

Alcuin also curated an extensive palace library, a priceless treasure in the time before the printing press. The library did more than simply house dusty old books that never saw the light of day. The new wave of literacy rocking Aachen was such that the library's books were in huge demand; scholars couldn't copy them fast enough.

Books themselves were also changed at Charlemagne's patronage. Writing was evolving, growing more and more accessible. Although it was once a skill reserved only for the most highly educated of people, reading was something that increasing numbers of noble-born people were able to do. This was in part thanks to education and in part thanks to the fact that Alcuin was revolutionizing the ease of reading by standardizing the use of capital letters and even spaces between words, inventing a new form of writing known as Carolingian minuscule.

Always the Christian king—even if he behaved more brutally than the so-called barbarians at times—Charlemagne encouraged Alcuin to work on the Bible, and the scholar quickly obliged. Many full editions of the Bible were copied and distributed all over the realm, and with Charlemagne's encouragement, the diverse peoples he ruled started to translate the Scriptures into their own vernacular. Saxons, Hispanics, Avars, and Slavs were all able to study the Bible in their own languages for the very first time.

The Bible was not the only ancient text that Charlemagne would preserve, however. In fact, the Carolingian Renaissance is responsible for the preservation of almost all the classical Latin texts we have today.

Without the printing press, producing books was an incredibly long and painstaking process. Every single line had to be copied by hand, word for word, often by quiet monks laboring away in their abbeys. The ancient Latin manuscripts were no exception, and in the dark years following the end of the Roman Empire, the war-torn world had seldom had the same time and money to copy them. But Charlemagne was determined to preserve every single one. He had hundreds of copies made of each of these important books, and in fact, almost all of the classical works we still have today were copied down by the Carolingians.

Without Charlemagne's influence, we wouldn't have Marcus Aurelius's *Meditations* or the *Aeneid*. We wouldn't know Tacitus's history of the Roman Empire or Julius Caesar's own account of his conquests in Gaul. Cicero's works would have been lost forever, and Pliny's *Natural History* would have disintegrated under the brutal weight of time.

This love of learning that was instilled across the Carolingian Empire was something that Charlemagne felt keenly in his own heart. He had summoned great masters from all over his realm to teach him various subjects harking back to ancient times, such as rhetoric, grammar, astronomy, logic, and even arithmetic. He became a learned man, far more so than most medieval kings, but there was one simple skill that many of us in the modern world take for granted, yet he could never master. Charlemagne could more than likely read, but he never did learn how to write. It hadn't been a part of his early education, and he tried to learn in later life, but the skill constantly eluded him.

The great emperor had conquered so many vast territories, yet he remained defeated by the written word. This appears to have frustrated him for decades. To the very end of his life, he kept a wax tablet under his pillow and would practice his letters in vain.

The Death of Charlemagne

As Charlemagne headed into his seventies, he began to cement the plans he'd made years before. Although many of his ideas were very progressive, Charlemagne was a traditionalist when it came to planning his succession. He considered his title as Holy Roman emperor to be something of an honorary thing, not tied to heredity, and so, he decided to split his lands among Charles, Pepin, and Louis.

Fate, however, had other ideas. In 810, the conflict with the Byzantine Empire came to a head. This empire controlled Venice, but the city had lost respect for Constantinople and switched its allegiance to Pepin, the king of Italy. The Byzantines would not give up Venice without a fight, though. Pepin rode to lay siege to the city, but his plans were doomed when disease broke out among his troops. He was forced to return to his own country with his tail between his legs and broken ranks of sick men. It is possible that Pepin himself had contracted an illness there, as he died just a few months later, leaving Italy without a king.

Just one year later, Charles the Younger, the king of Francia, suffered a similar tragedy. He was childless, and it was a horrific blow when he died in 811 after suffering from a stroke.

Bereaved of two cherished sons within a few months of one another, Charlemagne had to drag himself out of his personal grief to realize that their deaths could have terrible implications for his empire. At least he had one son left: Louis the Pious, the king of Aquitaine, who also controlled the Spanish Marches. Now that his brothers were dead, Louis would have to bear the full weight of the empire on his own young shoulders. In 813, possibly too old to travel to Rome, Charlemagne summoned Louis to meet him at Aachen. He had him anointed and crowned as co-emperor over the Carolingian Empire, although Louis would never be made Holy Roman emperor as his father had. Louis also received half of Charlemagne's lands; the emperor would leave the rest to him after his death, except for Italy, which went to Pepin's illegitimate son Bernard.

Charlemagne may have been growing too old and frail to ride all the way to Rome, but he still seemed to be fairly vigorous in the autumn of 813. He spent it hunting and riding in the beautiful, ardent countryside surrounding his peaceful home, safe in the knowledge that Louis was a man after his own heart and would care for the empire like it was his own. But disaster struck that winter. The emperor developed a cough and sudden fevers that would come and go, leaving his strong face haggard and pale.

By January, it was clear that Charlemagne was dying. He had contracted pleurisy, an inflammation of the spaces around the lungs, and in the 9th century, there was no way of treating it. On January 21st, 814, depressed beyond measure and still burning with ambition as much as he burned with fever, Charlemagne took to his bed. Seven days later, he died at the age of 71, having ruled over Francia for nearly half a century.

All of Charlemagne's personal wealth was donated to the Roman Catholic Church that he had protected so fervently during his lifetime.

Conclusion

As promised, upon the death of Charlemagne, Louis the Pious became the ruler over the Carolingian Empire, while Bernard became the king of Italy. And during the rule of Louis, the Carolingian Empire was held together, but it was a very tenuous bond. Louis would have been a much better clergyman than he was a king; he was a deeply devout person, devoted to the Church, and generally well-intentioned, but he failed miserably as an administrator. Several revolts occurred during his rule.

Things only worsened when Louis died, dividing the empire among his three sons. These men were jealous and ambitious, and they fought among one another, tearing the empire apart from the inside out. This made it vulnerable to attackers from beyond its borders. The Vikings, still clinging to their paganism and terrified of suffering the same fate as the Saxons, decided to strike first before they could be invaded. They annihilated the Carolingian Empire's borderlands and were perilously close to taking over Paris when the king of Francia—Charles the Fat, Charlemagne's great-grandson—bribed them to go away in 888. With that, the Carolingian Empire had fallen.

Yet the time of the Roman Empire itself was far from over. In fact, Charlemagne's coronation may have looked like a twitch in the death throes of Rome, but it was really the beginning of a whole new era. Nearly two centuries after the coronation of Charlemagne, a new Holy Roman emperor would be crowned when Otto I of Germany marched to the aid of Pope John XII. In gratitude, the pope gave him Charlemagne's ancient title, and the Roman Empire lived on as the Holy Roman Empire. It would remain an important force in world politics until its decline in 1806.

The Holy Roman Empire was not Charlemagne's only legacy. In fact, it is difficult to imagine a leader more influential in the course of history than this king with his conquests and his renaissance. There are many everyday aspects of our modern world that can be ascribed at least in part to his far-reaching influence. Our knowledge of ancient Rome. Our concept of modern-day Europe. The vast spread of Christianity and everything that came with it. Would more of us be celebrating Yuletide instead of Christmas if Charlemagne had never ruled?

This emperor was many things, and many of them were not positive. He was a murderer, a warrior. He was tempestuous, brutal, close-minded, and arrogant. But he was also intelligent, ambitious, driven, and determined. And like it or not, our lives today are very different because of this one man who lived more than a thousand years ago.

Sources

Kreis, S. 2006, *The Conversion of Clovis*, The History Guide, viewed 24 April 2020, <http://www.historyguide.org/ancient/clovis.html>

Rickard, J. 2012, *Battle of Soissons, 486*, History of War, viewed 24 April 2020, <http://www.historyofwar.org/articles/battles_soissons.html>

History.com Editors 2018, *Huns*, A&E Television Networks, viewed 15 April 2020, <https://www.history.com/topics/ancient-china/huns>

Pruitt, S. 2018, *8 Things You Might Not Know About Attila the Hun*, A&E Television Networks, viewed 15 April 2020, <https://www.history.com/news/8-things-you-might-not-know-about-attila-the-hun>

Pelegro, B. 2017, *Rome Halts the Huns*, National Geographic, viewed 15 April 2020, <https://www.nationalgeographic.com/history/magazine/2017/01-02/roman-empire-decline-attila-the-hun/>

Stoddard, B. C. 2014, *Attila the Hun & The Battle of the Catalaunian Plains*, Warfare History Network, viewed 15 April 2020, <https://warfarehistorynetwork.com/2014/08/27/attila-the-hun-the-battle-of-the-catalaunian-plains/>

Cavendish, R. 2011, *Death of Clovis I of the Franks*, History Today, viewed 15 April 2020, <https://www.historytoday.com/archive/death-clovis-i-franks>

Mingren, W. 2016, *The Commanding Clovis I: King of the Merovingian Dynasty and Founder of France*, Ancient Origins, viewed 15 April 2020, <https://www.ancient-origins.net/history-famous-people/commanding-clovis-i-king-merovingian-dynasty-and-founder-france-005777>

Violatti, C. 2014, *Franks*, Ancient History Encyclopedia, viewed 15 April 2020, <https://www.ancient.eu/Franks/>

Gascoigne, B. 2001, *History of the Franks*, viewed 15 April 2020, <http://www.historyworld.net/wrldhis/plaintexthistories.asp?historyid=ab74>

Wiener, J. 2013, *The Merovingians: The Kings and Queens of the Franks*, Ancient History Encyclopedia, viewed 15 April 2020, <https://etc.ancient.eu/interviews/the-merovingians-the-lords-and-ladies-of-the-dark-ages/>

Khan, S. M. 2020, *The Umayyad Dynasty*, Ancient History Encyclopedia, viewed 30 April 2020, <https://www.ancient.eu/Umayyad_Dynasty/>

History.com Editors 2019, *Battle of Tours*, A&E Television Networks, viewed 30 April 2020, <https://www.history.com/this-day-in-history/battle-of-tours>

Anonymous 2018, *Who Was Charles Martel and Why Is He Called the Hammer?*, History Hit, viewed 30 April 2020, <https://www.historyhit.com/day-charles-martel-dies/>

Hickman, K. 2019, *Biography of Charles Martel, Frankish Military Leader and Ruler*, ThoughtCo, viewed 30 April 2020, <https://www.thoughtco.com/muslim-invasions-charles-martel-2360687>

Shipley Duckett, E. 2019, *Pippin III*, Encyclopedia Britannica, viewed 30 April 2020, <https://www.britannica.com/biography/Pippin-III#ref5592>

Cybulskie, D. 2018, *Childhood in the Middle Ages*, Medievalists, viewed 30 April 2020, <https://www.medievalists.net/2018/11/childhood-middle-ages/>

Rendfeld, K. 2018, *Himiltrude: Charlemagne's First Ex-Wife*, Kim Rendfeld, viewed 1 May 2020, <https://kimrendfeld.wordpress.com/2018/09/12/himiltrude-charlemagnes-first-ex-wife/>

Schedel, H. 1493, *The Nuremberg Chronicle*, Morse Library, Beloit College, viewed 1 May 2020, <http://digicoll.library.wisc.edu/cgi/t/text/text-idx?c=nur;cc=nur;view=text;idno=nur.001.0004;rgn=div2;node=nur.001.0004%3A8.150>

Rendfeld, K. 2013, *The Last Lombard King*, Historical Fiction Research, viewed 3 June 2020, <http://historicalfictionresearch.blogspot.com/2013/01/the-last-lombard-king-kim-rendfeld.html>

Rendfeld, K. 2013, *Queen Mother Gerberga: Protecting Her Sons – And Her Power*, Kim Rendfeld, viewed 3 June 2020, <https://kimrendfeld.wordpress.com/2013/05/28/queen-mother-gerberga-protecting-her-sons-and-her-power/>

Rendfeld, K. 2012, *Family Feuds: Charlemagne and the Fate of the Church*, Unusual Historicals, viewed 3 June 2020, <http://unusualhistoricals.blogspot.com/2012/04/family-feuds-charlemagne-and-fate-of.html>

Rendfeld, K. 2013, *The Insulted Princess: Charlemagne's Second Wife*, Kim Rendfeld, viewed 3 June 2020, <https://kimrendfeld.wordpress.com/2013/12/18/the-insulted-princess-charlemagnes-second-wife/>

Snell, M. 2018, *The Lombards: A Germanic Tribe in Northern Italy*, ThoughtCo, viewed 3 June 2020, <https://www.thoughtco.com/the-lombards-defintion-1789086>

Mark, J. J. 2014, *Lombards*, Ancient History Encyclopedia, viewed 3 June 2020, <https://www.ancient.eu/Lombards/>

Anonymous 2015, *Ancient DNA cracks puzzle of Basque origins*, BBC News, viewed 4 June 2020, <https://www.bbc.com/news/science-environment-34175224>

Rodriguez, V. 2019, *Andorra*, Encyclopedia Britannica, viewed 4 June 2020, <https://www.britannica.com/place/Andorra>

Hickman, K. 2017, *Charlemagne: Battle of Roncevaux Pass*, ThoughtCo, viewed 4 June 2020, <https://www.thoughtco.com/charlemagne-battle-of-roncevaux-pass-2360883>

Sundqvist, O. 2015, *An Arena For Higher Powers: Ceremonial buildings and strategies for rulership in Late Iron Age Scandinavia*, BRILL via Google Books, viewed 5 June 2020, <https://books.google.co.za/books?id=CSdzCwAAQBAJ&dq=irminsul+pillar&source=gbs_navlinks_s>

Anonymous 2020, *Paganism, Anglo-Saxon*, Encyclopedia.com, viewed 5 June 2020, <https://www.encyclopedia.com/environment/encyclopedias-almanacs-transcripts-and-maps/paganism-anglo-saxon>

Packer, J. I. 2000, *131 Christians Everyone Should Know*, Holman Reference

Sass, R. 2018, *Saxon Paganism for Today*, Lulu Press, Inc. via Google Books, viewed 5 June 2020, <https://books.google.co.za/books?id=OZg6CgAAQBAJ&dq=fritzlar+church+saxon+burn&source=gbs_navlinks_s>

Violatti, C. 2014, *The Saxons*, Ancient History Encyclopedia, viewed 5 June 2020, <https://www.ancient.eu/Saxons/>

Anonymous 2018, *Widukind, Saxon thorn*, The Eighth Century and All That, viewed 5 June 2020, <http://www.8thcentury.com/widukind-saxon-thorn/>

Anonymous 2018, *Saxon Wars I*, The Eighth Century and All That, viewed 5 June 2020, <http://www.8thcentury.com/the-saxon-wars-i-lets-do-this/>

Anonymous 2018, *Saxon Wars 2: Charles, lawgiver and butcher*, The Eighth Century and All That, viewed 5 June 2020, <http://www.8thcentury.com/saxon-wars-2-charles-lawgiver-and-butcher/>

Anonymous 2018, *Saxon Wars 3: The war is over! Right?*, The Eighth Century and All That, viewed 5 June 2020, <http://www.8thcentury.com/saxon-wars-3-the-war-is-over-right/>

Evans, G. R. 2014, *Charlemagne vs. the Saxons*, Christian History Magazine, viewed 5 June 2020, <https://christianhistoryinstitute.org/magazine/article/charlemagne-vs-the-saxons>

Hourly History 2016, *Charlemagne: A Life from Beginning to End*, Hourly History via Google Books, viewed 5 June 2020, <https://books.google.co.za/books?id=9JKeDwAAQBAJ&dq=battle+of+trsat&source=gbs_navlinks_s>

Story, J. 2005, *Charlemagne: Empire and Society*, Manchester University Press via Google Books, viewed 5 June 2020, <https://books.google.co.za/books?id=vTbvq_8HFPUC&dq=charlemagne+slavs&source=gbs_navlinks_s>

Violatti, C. 2014, *Slavs*, Ancient History Encyclopedia, viewed 5 June 2020, <https://www.ancient.eu/Slavs/>

Mark, J. J. 2014, *Avars*, Ancient History Encyclopedia, viewed 5 June 2020, <https://www.ancient.eu/Avars/>

Pohl, W. 2018, *What is So Fascinating About the Avars?*, Osterreichische Akademie der Wissenschaften, viewed 5 June 2020,

<https://www.oeaw.ac.at/imafo/read/article/what-is-so-fascinating-about-the-avars/>

Bachrach, B. 2013, *Charlemagne's Early Campaigns (768-777): A Diplomatic and Military Analysis*, BRILL via Google Books, viewed 5 June 2020, <https://books.google.co.za/books?id=k0B92eRh2-EC&dq=charlemagne+bavaria&source=gbs_navlinks_s>

Anonymous 2020, *Louis I*, Encyclopedia.com, viewed 6 June 2020, <https://www.encyclopedia.com/people/history/french-history-biographies/louis-i-louis-pious>

Editors of the Encyclopedia Britannica 2019, *Carolingian dynasty*, Encyclopedia Britannica, viewed 6 June 2020, <https://www.britannica.com/topic/Carolingian-dynasty>

Freeman, J. A. 2014, *Alcuin of York*, Christian History Institute, viewed 6 June 2020, <https://christianhistoryinstitute.org/magazine/article/alcuin-of-york-and-charlemagne>

Fleener, M. 2005, *The Significance of the Coronation of Charlemagne*, Medievalists, viewed 6 June 2020, <https://www.medievalists.net/2010/12/the-significance-of-the-coronation-of-charlemagne/>

von Hellfold, M. 2009, *Charlemagne is crowned emperor – December 25, 800*, DW.com, viewed 6 June 2020, <https://www.dw.com/en/charlemagne-is-crowned-emperor-december-25-800/a-4614858-1>

Loughlin, J. 1907, *Pope Adrian I*, Catholic Encyclopedia, viewed 6 June 2020, <https://www.newadvent.org/cathen/01155b.htm>

Editors of the Encyclopedia Britannica 2020, *Adrian I*, Encyclopedia Britannica, viewed 6 June 2020, <https://www.britannica.com/biography/Adrian-I>

Mann, H. 1910, *Pope St. Leo III*, Catholic Encyclopedia, viewed 6 June 2020, <https://www.newadvent.org/cathen/09157b.htm>

Snell, M. 2017, *Pope Leo III*, Thoughtco, viewed 6 June 2020, <https://www.thoughtco.com/pope-leo-iii-profile-1789101>

Editors of the Encyclopedia Britannica 2020, *Pippin, King of Italy*, Encyclopedia Britannica, viewed 6 June 2020, <https://www.britannica.com/biography/Pippin-king-of-Italy>

Sullivan, R. E. 2020, *Charlemagne*, Encyclopedia Britannica, viewed 6 June 2020, <https://www.britannica.com/biography/Charlemagne/Military-campaigns>

Biography.com Editors 2014, *Charlemagne*, Biography.com, viewed 6 June 2020, <https://www.biography.com/royalty/charlemagne>

Brondou, C. 2011, *Charlemagne, King of the Franks and Holy Roman Emperor*, Finding Dulcinea, viewed June 2020, <http://www.findingdulcinea.com/features/profiles/c/charlemagne.html>

History.com Editors 2019, *Charlemagne*, A&E Television Networks, viewed June 2020, <https://www.history.com/topics/middle-ages/charlemagne>

Mark, J. J. 2019, *Charlemagne*, Ancient History Encyclopedia, viewed June 2020, <https://www.ancient.eu/Charlemagne/>

Illustration I:
https://commons.wikimedia.org/wiki/File:Charlemagne_Notre_Dame.jpg

Illustration II:
https://commons.wikimedia.org/wiki/File:Charlemagne_and_Pope_Adrian_I.jpg

Illustration III:
https://commons.wikimedia.org/wiki/File:Ary_Scheffer,_Charlemagne_re%C3%A7oit_la_soumission_de_Widukind_%C3%A0_Paderborn,_(1840).jpg

Here's another book by Captivating History
that you might be interested in

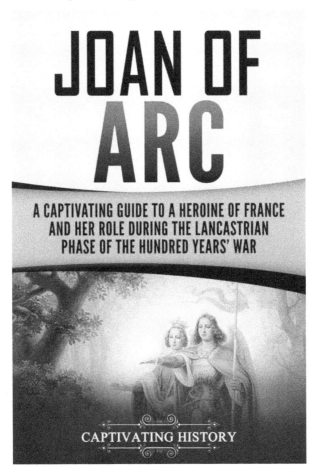

CPSIA information can be obtained
at www.ICGtesting.com
Printed in the USA
BVHW040850191222
654533BV00002B/82

9 781647 488550